A NATURALIST'S GUIDE TO THE

BIRDS
OF
NEPAL

Bhutan and Northeast India

Bikram Grewal

JOHN BEAUFOY PUBLISHING

First published in the United Kingdom in 2023 by John Beaufoy Publishing

11 Blenheim Court, 316 Woodstock Road, Oxford OX2 7NS, England

www.johnbeaufoy.com

10 9 8 7 6 5 4 3 2 1

Photo Credits

Front cover: *main image* Fire-tailed Myzornis (Clement M Francis), *bottom left* Satyr Tragopan (Arpit Deomurari), *bottom centre* Rock Bunting (Garima Bhatia), *bottom right* Little Ringed Plover (Nitin Srinivasamurthy).
Back cover: Kalij Pheasant (Arpit Deomurari). **Title page:** Coal Tit (Amit Sharma).
Contents page: Little Pied Flycatcher (Gururaj Moorching)
Main descriptions: photos are denoted by a page number followed by T (top), B (bottom), L (left), R (right), a (above), b (below).

A V Prassana: 71B, 94TR; **Abhishek Das:** 69B, 135B; **Amano Samarpan:** 65B; **Amit Thakurta:** 75BR, 135TR, 143BL; **Arpit Bansal:** 47BL, 58T, 77B, 85B; **Arpit Deomurari:** 17T, 18T, 39T, 44BR, 89B, 98T, 132BL, 133TbR, 137BRb; **Bhanu Singh:** 16B, 60T; **Bikram Grewal:** 47T; **Bishan Monappa:** 39BL, 52TR, 54BR, 69TL, 74TR, 75BL, 88B, 115BL, 133TbL, 133B, 134BR; **Biswapriya Rahut:** 83BR; **Clement M Francis:** 14TL, 14B, 20T, 23B, 24B, 25B, 26TR, 26BR, 30T, 31TL, 31B, 32B, 37BR, 43B, 46T, 48T, 64T, 76T, 77TR, 90TL, 91T, 96T, 99B, 100BR, 102Bb, 108T, 127BL; **Devashish Deb:** 106T; **Dhritiman Hore:** 87T, 149BL; **Dolly Bhardwaj:** 130TR, **Garima Bhatia:** 14TR, 17BR, 18B, 22T, 22Ba, 29TL, 29BL, 33B, 34TR, 35B, 37T, 37BL, 40Ta, 41Ba, 42TR, 43T, 44T, 44BL, 49T, 49B, 50T, 50B, 51T, 51BR, 52TL, 53T, 54T, 54BL, 56BL, 57TL, 57TR, 57B, 59TR, 59TL, 60B, 61T, 62T, 62BL, 62BR, 63T, 64B, 65T, 66BL, 67TL, 67B, 68T, 70T, 71T, 72T, 72B, 73TL, 73TR, 73B, 74TL, 74B, 76B, 77TL, 79TL, 79TR, 80TL, 80BL, 80BC, 81BL, 81BR, 82Ta, 82Tb, 82BL, 82BR, 83TR, 83TL, 84T, 85TR, 86T, 89T, 90B, 92B, 93B, 94BL, 94BR, 96BR, 97B, 98BL, 99TR, 100T, 100BL, 101T, 101B, 102T, 102Ba, 103T, 104T, 105T, 106B, 107B, 108B, 110T, 111TR, 111TL, 111BL, 112T, 114T, 115T, 115BR, 116T, 116B, 117TL, 118T, 119BL, 120TL, 120B, 121T, 121B, 122Ta, 122BL, 122BR, 123TR, 123TL, 123B, 124B, 125T, 126TL, 126TR, 126BL, 126BC, 127BR, 128TL, 128TR, 128Ba, 128Bb, 129TL, 129TR, 129BL, 129BR, 130TL, 130BL, 130BR, 131BR, 131BL, 132T, 134T, 134BL, 136T, 136B, 137T, 137BL, 138Ta, 138Tb, 138BR, 139TL, 139TR, 139B, 140TL, 140B, 141T, 141B, 142T, 143T, 143BR, 144TL, 144B, 145BC, 145BL, 146TL, 146TR, 146B, 147T, 147BL, 147BR, 148TL, 148TRa, 148TRb, 148BL, 148BR, 149T, 150TL, 150TR, 150B; **Gopinath Kollur:** 19B; **Gunjan Arora:** 26TL, 91BR, 151T; **Gururaj Moorching:** 26BL, 28BL, 66TL, 127T, 131T; **Jainy Maria Kurikose:** 12B, 28BR, 36TR, 45BL, 55Tb, 56BR, 109B, 112B, 135TL; **Jugul Tiwari:** 59BRa; **Jyotendra Thakuri:** 12T; **Kintoo Dhawan:** 13T; **Kshounish Shankar Ray:** 40BL, 96BL, 144TR; **Kunan Naik:** 21T, 30B, 40Tb, 41Bb, 42TL, 42B, 83BL, 86BR; **Maitreyee Das:** 132BR; **Manjula Mathur:** 66BR; **Meg Roy Choudhury:** 107T, 117Bb; **Mousumi Datta:** 94TL; **Nikhil Devasar:** 27B, 28T, 35T, 38BL, 41Tb, 45T, 46BL, 51BL, 55B, 61B, 88TL, 111BR, 124T, 126BR, 138BL, 151BL; **Ninaad Kulkarni:** 137BRa; **Niranjan Sant:** 40BR, 59BRb, 95B, 97T; **Nitin Bhardwaj:** 19T, 45BR; **Nitin Srinivasamurthy:** 27TL, 29BR, 29TR, 32T, 34B, 38T, 39BR, 41Ta, 52B, 53B, 80BR, 90TR, 93T, 99TL, 114B, 117TR, 122Tb, 133Ta 140TR, 142BL, 149BR; **Prasad Basavaraj:** 103B; **Prashant Poojary:** 58B; **Prassana Parab:** 24T; **Pushpal Goswami:** 88TR; **Rahul Sharma:** 15T; **Rajat Bhargava:** 67TR, 78T; **Rajneesh Suvarna:** 56TL, 56TR, 119BR; **Ramki Sreenivasan:** 15B, 34TL, 55Ta, 87B, 91BL, 95TR, 109T, 113T; **Rathika Ramasami:** 25T; **Roon Bhuyan:** 36B; **Samyak Kaninde:** 66TR; **SarwanDeep Singh:** 48B, 98BR, 113B; **Satyendra Sharma:** 13B; **Sharad Sridhar:** 145BR; **Siddhesh Bramhankar:** 27TR; **Suboranjan Sen:** 17BL, 20B, 46BR, 47BR, 59BL, 68B; **Sujan Chatterjee:** 120TR; **Sumit Das:** 16T; **Sumit K Sen:** 21B, 31TR, 36TL, 69TR, 75T, 80TR, 86BL, 125B; **Supriyo Samanta:** 22Bb, 33T, 81T; **Tapas Misra:** 23T.

ISBN 978-1-912081-39-4

Edited by Krystyna Mayer and typeset by Alpana Khare Graphic Design, New Delhi, India
Printed and bound in Malaysia by Times Offset (M) Sdn. Bhd.

·CONTENTS·

INTRODUCTION

Oblong and slightly bigger than England, Greece or New Zealand, Nepal runs east to west along the spine of the Himalayas and contains eight of the world's tallest mountain peaks. These mountains, including the formidable Mount Everest at 8,775m, and dozens of smaller peaks, pierce a cobalt-blue sky. They hem in tiny towns, villages and hamlets with the residents' huts dotted across the landscape and clinging precariously to the steep hillsides. These daunting mountain barriers for years walled out the world, thereby ensuring Nepal's independence and preserving its forests and its flora and fauna. The Himalayan region displays great variety in flora and fauna. It is also where rare medicinal herbs are said to grow. In the terai (foothills), there are luxuriant tropical forests of sal, teak and shisham. Higher up there are varieties of chir (pine), oak, deodar, fir, rhododendron, birch and juniper. At higher altitudes the juniper becomes a bush. Where the tree-line ends, the alpine meadows begin to unfold like a green velvet carpet. Himalayan flowers of rare beauty are seen in abundance, their soft petals adorned with raindrops reflecting the delicate hues of sunrise and sunset.

It is difficult to imagine today that these Himalayan slopes were densely wooded less than a century ago. E. T. Atkinson in his Gazetteer mentioned coniferous forests that reminded him of 'unbroken masses' swelling like waves of the sea over many miles, and presenting a scene of magnificent grandeur unknown elsewhere.

For a country so small in size, Nepal is incredibly rich in its avifauna. This is in part due to its terrain, habitat, climate and altitudinal variation. Three-quarters of Nepal is mountains, with the rest being flatlands that run along its borders with India. With more than 850 bird species recorded in this tiny country, it is no wonder that birders from all over the world flock to see its raptors, pheasants, snowcocks and small Himalayan seed-eaters. The Spiny Babbler is Nepal's only endemic. Fast and furious rives, including the Kosi, Gandaki, Goghra and Mahakali, rise in the mighty Himalayas and drain south into India. These rivers, along with adequate rainfall, ensure furious plant growth, which in turn provides abundant nourishment. Nepal can be roughly divided into four regions.

OUTER TERAI

This remarkable flat, low-altitude strip running along Nepal's southern borders belies the belief that the country consists only of mountains. In economic terms it produces 60 per cent of the grain despite being only a fifth of the country, and houses more than 50 per cent of the population. Terai, which means 'marshy' in Persian, forms the northern extension of the Gangetic Plain and varies between 20 and 30km in width. This is a rich agricultural belt that stretches along the southern part of the terai, and it is Nepal's most economically important region. The topsoil here is replenished annually with the waters of the many streams and rivulets that run down the hills, making it the food bowl that feeds the agriculturally deficient hill regions. The Outer Terai ends at the base of foothills – the Sivaliks or the Churia, as they are locally called.

A tropical moist zone of deciduous vegetation occurs in the terai and the Churia Range. The forests consist mainly of khair *Acacia catechu*, sissoo *Dalbergia sissoo* and sal *Shorea*

Terai landscape

robusta. A remarkably flat, low-altitude strip running along Nepal's southern border, the terai contradicts the national image of mountains, mountains and more mountains, but it is doubtful whether the country could exist without it. Seldom wider than 48km, with an average altitude of 150m above sea level, the terai can be divided into two regions: the flat Outer Terai running along the Indian border, and the Inner Terai, a higher, bumpier zone sandwiched between two sets of Himalayan foothills, the Siwalik and Mahabharat ranges. Geographically, the terai is an extension of India's great Gangetic Plain, and its customs and languages are heavily influenced by Indian culture. The indigenous residents are the Tharu, a handsome, gentle people who tend to be dominated by later arrivals. These ethnic groups are largely ignored by tourists as well as by the mainstream Bahun-Chhetri who run Nepal, but they constitute about a quarter of the total population.

The northern region, which adjoins the foothills, is often referred to as Bhabhar, named after the tall grass *Eulaliopsis binate* that grows here. Once it was a malarial belt, but this is less the case now due to the widespread use of DDT.

INNER TERAI

Above the Bhabhar belt, the Sivaliks/Churia Range has peaks as high as 1,000m. In several places lie broad basins, or 'dun' valleys, which have rich agricultural soil. Once these too were malarial except to the local Tharu people, who seem to have acquired a natural resistance. Verdant with lush grassland and sal forests that rise to 40m, these forests are home to a diverse animal population, including the tiger. Many parts have now been cleared to provide timber and increase the area for cultivation. The terai is best visited in autumn or winter, when clear days reveal startling vistas of the distant Himalayas rising behind fields. The period following the annual grass-cutting season in January is considered the best.

THE MID-MOUNTAIN REGION

Between the Mahabharat Range and the high Himalayas are ranges that vary in height between 2,440 and 4.270m, with sharp slopes towards the south and more gentle slopes to the north. These hills are also the cultural heartland of Nepal and Kathmandu, and the Pokhara valleys lie in this region. Once dotted with lakes, the valleys were formed by deposits of fluvial material brought down by rivers and glaciers from the surrounding ranges.

Mahabharat range

At elevations between 1,525 and 3,050m, the vegetation comprises mainly pines, oaks, rhododendrons, poplars, walnuts and larch. At 3,050–3,660m, fir mixed with birch and rhododendron can be found. The large forested tracts below the timber-line consist of some of the most valuable forests of spruce, fir, cypress, juniper and birch. These areas are virtually uninhabited.

HIGH HIMALAYAS

Nepal's northern border is lined by an unbroken 50km-wide strip of high mountain peaks. The Himalayas, literally 'the abode of snow' in traditional Sanskrit, are the world's highest mountains; they are also the world's youngest mountains, growing at about 10–12cm a year. Behind the mighty range rises the flat, rainless Tibetan Plateau. It is also the source of several mighty rivers.

Mt Everest

The mountains range in elevation between 4,265m and more than 8,840m, and include many of the world's highest peaks – Everest, Kanchenjunga, Lhotse I, Makalu I, Cho Oyu, Dhaulagiri I, Manaslu I and Annapurna I – all of them above 7,925m. Except for scattered settlements in high mountain valleys, this entire area is uninhabited. Alpine vegetation occurs in the higher regions, just below the snow-line, with low scrub vegetation, making it a grazing ground in the summer.

Habitat

While many common species are spread over large areas of the Oriental realm, others are limited not just to a region but also to habitat. Some birds of the conifer forests of the hills are found only there, while grassland birds may be restricted to that habitat.

As Nepal has a very dense human population, birds that get on well with man flourish here. They are not limited to House Sparrows, crows and House Martins. Subcontinental culture has traditionally respected all forms of life, and protected birds before sanctuaries and parks were ever thought of. India's only resident crane, the Sarus Crane, is left unharmed no matter how much of a farmer's pea crop it consumes. The Indian Peafowl has semi-sacred status in some areas, which is why it is found in large numbers undisturbed. The Red Junglefowl has a long history of association with humans and is the ancestor of the domestic chicken.

City gardens provide homes for many species, including tailorbirds, sunbirds, white-eyes, babblers and the ubiquitous myna. Other birds take advantage of cultivation techniques, especially Indian Pond Herons, which often take up position in paddy fields, practising what villagers call *bagla bhakti* – supreme hypocrisy: sitting like a holy man lost in meditation, but in fact just waiting to stab something in the back. Little Grebes also take up residence in village ponds, while refuse is in great demand by pariah kites that, along with pariah dogs, haunt the rubbish heaps of the subcontinent.

Shallow lagoons, inland jheels, or shallow lakes, and rivers are rich habitats for waterbirds from pelicans, storks, cranes, egrets and cormorants, to jacanas and gallinules among the lotuses, and waders that pick their way along the water's edge probing for food. Huge numbers of migratory waterfowl also congregate at jheels during the winter months. Other birds, like bitterns, conceal themselves among reed beds. Numerous birds of prey can also be found near water.

Forest birds are more difficult to spot, especially when they are concealed in the tree canopy. However, they can often be seen in clearings flying from tree to tree, or on the edges of forests where the sun can penetrate and there is a great deal of insect activity. Often assorted species form hunting parties and move together through the forest. Thus in a single place you can see woodpeckers, warblers, tits and treecreepers. Often birds can be located and identified by their calls. Here it is also worth noting that Nepal forests are home to many more birds than those nearer either pole. A tropical forest can hold over 200 bird species at more than 5,000 pairs per kilometre, but a northern forest may hold fewer than 20 species at 200 individuals per kilometre. The Himalayas are home to several species of tit, accentors and also birds of prey like griffons and buzzards.

WHERE TO SEE BIRDS IN NEPAL

Chitwan National Park was established as a national park in 1973, and granted World Heritage Site status in 1984. It covers an area of 932km and is located in the subtropical Inner Terai lowlands of south-central Nepal in the districts of Nawalparasi, Chitwan and Makwanpur. It ranges in altitude from about 100m in the river valleys to 815m in the Churia Hills.

In the north and west of the protected area, the Narayani Rapti River forms a natural boundary to human settlements. Adjacent to the east of the park is **Parsa Wildlife Reserve**, and contiguous in the south is the Indian tiger reserve of **Valmiki National Park**. The coherent protected area of 2,075km represents the Tiger Conservation Unit of Chitwan-Parsa, which covers 3,549km^2 and is a huge block of alluvial grassland and subtropical moist deciduous forests. Among the most sought after birds here are Great and Oriental Pied Hornbills, and the Red-Headed Trogon, Hooded Pitta and Grey-crowned Prinia.

Royal Bardia National Park in western Nepal is less known but is perhaps a better alternative to Chitwan. Similar in terrain, it covers approximately 1,000km² of forested hills and grassland, interspersed with water channels. It started life as a royal hunting ground but was later (in 1988)

Chitwan National Park

declared a national park. Along with the adjoining **Banke National Park**, it is probably the largest and most undisturbed park in the terai. About 70 per cent of it is forested, and the rest is a mix of grassland and riverine forest. Best known for its birds (about 400 species), it is also rich in mammals. Birds seen here include the Great Slaty Woodpecker and Lesser Adjutant.

Royal Shukhlaphanta Wildlife Reserve consists of one of the most remote but largest extant grasslands typical of the region. Once a famous hunting ground, it is known for its extensive herds of the vulnerable Swamp Deer, tigers and elephants. It is difficult to reach and extensive planning is required to visit it. Interesting birds here include the vulnerable Swamp Francolin and the highly endangered Bengal Florican.

Kosi Tappu Wildlife Reserve is located in the floodplains of eastern terai, on the Saptakoshi River. It is an excellent place to see migratory Asian waterbirds, including the rare Baer's Pochard and Falcated Duck.

Annapurna Conservation Area suffers as it is located along Nepal's most popular trekking route, with several trails following the small and narrow path leading to the sanctuary, which in itself is surrounded by towering peaks – Hiuchuli, Annapurna South, Annapurna I and II, Fang and Machhapuchhare. The vegetation consists of temperate rhodedendron and oak forests, some bamboo forests and high-altitude grassland. This is a good place to see the Yellow-rumped Honeyguide, and excellent for seeing different vulture species.

Langtang National Park is situated in the central Himalayas, and is the nearest park to Kathmandu. The area extends from 32km north of Kathmandu. Langtang was designated as the first Himalayan national park in 1970–71, and was gazetted in March 1976. The park protects a high Himalayan valley that stretches north from Helambu all the way to the Tibetan border.

Sagarmatha National Park covers an area of 1,148km² in Nepal's Khumbu region. The park includes the highest peak in the world, Mt Sagarmatha (Everest 8,848m) and several other well-known peaks such as Lhotse, Cho Oyu, Pumori, Ama Dablam, Thamerku, Kwangde, Kangtaiga and Gyachyung Kang.

Vegetation in the park varies from pine and hemlock forests at lower altitudes, fir, juniper, birch and rhododendron woods at mid-elevations, scrub and alpine plant communities higher up, and bare rock and snow above the tree-line. The famed blooming of rhododendrons occurs during spring, although much of the flora is most colourful during the monsoon season (June–August). The park provides a habitat for several bird species. The most common ones to be seen include the Himalayan Monal (the national bird of Nepal), Blood and Cheer Pheasants, Alpine and Yellow-billed Choughs, Snow Pigeon, Himalayan Griffon, Lammergier and Snow Partridge.

Dhorpatan Hunting Reserve lies in the Rukum, Myagdi and Baglung districts in the Dhaulagiri Himal Range in West Nepal. Putha, Churen and Gurja Himal extend over the northern boundary of the reserve. Dhorpatan Hunting Reserve was established in 1983 and gazetted in 1987.

Phulchowki, though not a designated park, is located in the southern part of the Kathmandu Valley. The 2,782m-high mountain, along with the Godavari Botanical Gardens, is one of the most convenient and best places to watch a wide range of birds, including the Black-faced Warbler, Himalayan Cutia and Yellow-bellied Flowerpecker.

The Makalu Barun National Park and Conservation Area was established in 1992 as Nepal's eighth national park and the first to include the adjacent inhabited conservation area as a buffer. High in the heart of the eastern Himalayas, seven valleys radiate from Mt Makalu, the world's fifth highest peak. These valleys, particularly the Barun Valley, contain some of the last remaining pristine forests and alpine meadows of Nepal. From the bottom of the Arun Valley at just 435m above sea level, the Himalayas rise to the snow-capped tip of Makalu (8,463m), within a 40km distance. In this wide range of altitudes and climates, the Makalu-Barun area contains some of the richest and most diverse pockets of plants and animals in Nepal. Birds include Gould's Shortwing, and the Black-throated Parrotbill and Purple Cochoa.

Rara National Park is located in north-west Nepal and is about 371km by air from Kathmandu. The park headquarters is about 32km north to Jumla. Most of the park, including Lake Rara, lies in Mugu district, with a small area in the Jumla district of the Karnali Zone. This is the smallest park in Nepal (106km^2) with the country's biggest lake, and is excellent for migratory wildfowl.

Kanchenjunga Conservation Area is located below Mt Kanchenjunga (8,586m). Spread across an area of 2,035km^2, the area is made up of alpine grassland, rocky outcrops, dense temperate and subtropical forests, and low river valleys, with the looming Kanchenjunga as its crown. Situated in north-eastern Nepal in Taplejung district, the conservation area is bordered by the Tibet Autonomous Region-China in the north, Sikkim-India in the east and Sankhuwasabha district in the west. In 1998, the Department of National Parks and Wildlife Conservation and WWF Programme jointly launched the Kanchenjunga Conservation Area Project to implement biodiversity conservation and sustainable development in the area.

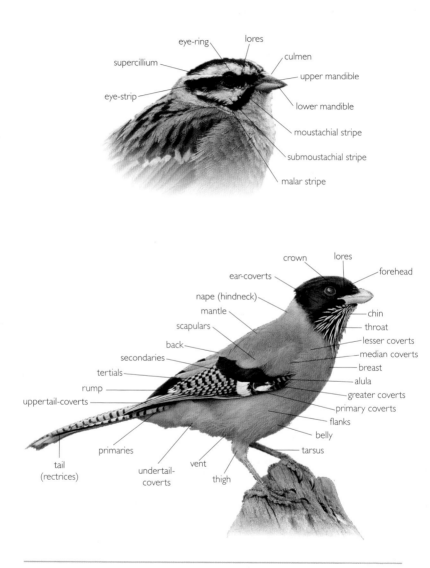

aberrant Abnormal or unusual
adult Mature; capable of breeding
aerial Making use of the open sky
aquatic Living on or in water
arboreal Living in trees
canopy Leafy foliage of treetops
casque Growth above bill of hornbills
cheek Term loosely applied to sides of head, below the eye or on ear-coverts
collar Distinctive band of colour that encircles or partly encircles neck
coverts Small feathers on wings, ears and base of tail
crepuscular Active at dusk and dawn
crest Extended feathers on head
crown-stripe Distinct line from forehead along centre of crown
duars Forest areas S of E Himalayas
ear-coverts Feathers covering the ear opening. Often distinctly coloured
endemic Indigenous and confined to a place
eye-ring Contrasting ring around eye
extinct No longer in existence
family Specified group of genera
forage Search for food
flank Side of body
foreneck Lower throat
form Subspecies
gape Basal part of beak
genus Group of related species
jheel Shallow lake or wetland
hackles Long and pointed neck feathers
hepatic Rust-or liver-coloured plumage phase, mainly in female cuckoos
iris Coloured eye membrane surrounding pupil
lanceolate Lance-shaped; slim and pointed
malar Stripe on side of throat
mandible Each of the two parts of bill
mantle Back, between wings
mask Dark plumage around eyes and ear-coverts
morph One of several distinct types of plumage in the same species
moult Seasonal shedding of plumage
nocturnal Active at night
nominate First subspecies to be formally named
non-passerine All orders of birds except for passerines

nullah Ditch or stream bed, dry or wet
order Group of related families
palearctic Old World and arctic zone
pelagic Ocean-going
pied Black and white
plumage Feathers of a bird
primaries Outer flight feathers in wing
race Subspecies
range Geographical area or areas inhabited by a species
raptors Birds of prey and vultures, excluding owls
rump Lower back
scapulars Feathers along edge of mantle
secondaries Inner wing feathers
sholas Small forests in valleys
speculum Area of colour on secondary feathers of wings
streamers Long extensions to feathers, usually of tail
spangles Distinctive white or shimmering spots in plumage
species Groups of birds reproductively isolated from other such groups
storey Level of a tree or forest
subspecies Distinct form that does not have specific status
supercilium Streak above eye
talons Strong, sharp claws used to seize or kill prey
terai Alluvial land S of Himalayas
tarsus Lower part of a bird's legs
terminal band Broad band on tip of feather or tail
tertials Innermost wing-coverts, often covering secondaries
underparts Undersurface of a bird from throat to vent
underwing Undersurface of a wing including linings and flight feathers
upperparts Upper surface of a bird including wings, back and tail
vagrant Accidental, irregular
vent Undertail area
wing-coverts Small feathers on wing at bases of primaries and secondaries
wingspan Length from one wing tip to the other when fully extended
winter plumage Plumage seen during non-breeding winter months

Snow Partridge ■ *Lerwa lerwa* 38cm

DESCRIPTION Plump, high-altitude, medium-sized game bird with red bill and legs. Vermiculated black and white on head and upperparts. White below with heavy chestnut

streaking. Short tail. Sexes alike. **FOOD** Moss, lichens, seeds, ferns and rhododendrons. **VOICE** Repeated low whistle. **DISTRIBUTION** Local breeding resident in northern mountains from N Pakistan east to Arunachal Pradesh. Moves lower down in winter. Also C Asia and China. **HABITAT & HABITS** Inhabits steep, rocky or grassy slopes near snowline. Feeds in pairs or small parties (coveys) on the ground. Very confiding where not hunted, often watching observer from rock. When disturbed flies downhill with clattering wings. Nests on the ground.

Tibetan Snowcock
■ *Tetraogallus tibetanus* 51cm

DESCRIPTION Large, plump, high-altitude game bird with chestnut rump and tail. Grey-streaked white above, with darker neck, crown and face-stripes, and white cheeks and throat. White below with bold black flank-stripes. White secondaries obvious in flight. Sexes alike. **FOOD** Shoots, leaves, roots, berries and insects. **VOICE** Noisy. Accelerating bubbling, whistle and *cur lee* call. **DISTRIBUTION** Fairly common disjunct breeding resident in northern mountains from Ladakh to Arunachal Pradesh. Winters lower down. Also Tibet and China. **HABITAT & HABITS** Inhabits rocky ridges, slopes and meadows above snowline. Feeds actively on the ground in pairs or coveys. Cocks tail. Runs uphill or flies a long distance down when disturbed. Nests on the ground.

Chukar ■ *Alectoris chukar* 38cm

DESCRIPTION Plump, medium-sized, dry-country game bird with zebra-striped flanks. Pale sandy-grey above; greyer on breast, tail and lower back. Chestnut outer tail. Creamy throat surrounded by black line. Prominent flank-stripes and warm buff belly. Red bill and legs. Sexes alike. **FOOD** Seeds, roots, shoots, insects and succulent vegetation. **VOICE** Loud, rapidly repeated *chukchukchuk*. **DISTRIBUTION** Locally common breeding resident in northern mountains from western Pakistan east to Nepal. Very rare in accessible parts of Pakistan due to hunting. Some move lower down in winter. Also E Europe, W and C Asia, and China. **HABITAT & HABITS** Inhabits dry, stony and rocky hillsides, and terraced cultivation. Feeds in pairs or coveys on the ground. Runs rapidly. Flies fast and low on whirring wings, usually downhill. Not shy where unmolested, often perching prominently on rocks. Males aggressive to each other when breeding. Nests on the ground.

Tibetan Partridge
■ *Perdix hodgsoniae* 31cm

DESCRIPTION Medium-sized, high-altitude game bird with black cheeks. Richly buff, barred brown above. Chestnut neck and flanks; heavily black barred and blotched on breast and belly. White throat, supercilia and upper neck contrasting with black eye-stripes and cheek-patches. Sexes similar. North-western race (shown) paler. **FOOD** Seeds, shoots and insects. **VOICE** Call a rattling, repeated *scherrrreck* and a high *chee chee chee*. **DISTRIBUTION** Locally common breeding resident in N India, Nepal and Bhutan along border with Tibet. Also C Asia and China. **HABITAT & HABITS** Inhabits high-altitude semi-desert and rocky slopes with scattered low scrub. Feeds on the ground in pairs or coveys. Runs rapidly uphill when disturbed or flies downhill.

Black Francolin ■ *Francolinus francolinus* 34cm

DESCRIPTION Dark, medium-sized game bird. Male: buff-edged dark brown above including crown, barred paler on rump and tail; chestnut undertail; black below with heavy white spotting, white cheeks and broad chestnut collar. Female: duller; streaked brown above; white-edged black below with chestnut hindneck. **FOOD** Grain, seeds, shoots, tubers, fallen berries and insects. **VOICE** Noisy. Rather soft but far-carrying call, *chik chirrik cheek chereek* with variations, preceded by distinct *clik* at short range. **DISTRIBUTION**

Locally common breeding resident in northern plains and low hills from Pakistan east to NE India including Nepal. Very rare in Bangladesh. Replaced in Deccan by next species. Also W Asia. **HABITAT & HABITS** Inhabits reed beds and irrigated cultivation, particularly sugar cane, tall grass and scrub near water. Feeds in pairs or coveys on the ground. Shy and secretive but often calls from high perch. Rather crepuscular.

Hill Partridge ■ *Arborophila torqueola* 28cm

DESCRIPTION Medium-sized, dark forest game bird with bright chestnut head. Black barred brown above. Grey below with chestnut and white flank-streaks. Bright chestnut head with white-streaked black eye-stripes, throat and neck. White neck collar. Female

dull with brownish head. **FOOD** Seeds, shoots, berries, insects and small molluscs; also larvae. **VOICE** Rather eerie, repeated whistle, *po eer, po eer*. Also rapid *kwikkwikkwik*. **DISTRIBUTION** Fairly common breeding resident in northern mountains from Himachal Pradesh to Myanmar border. Also Tibet and SE Asia. **HABITAT & HABITS** Inhabits the ground of well-forested slopes and ravines, feeding in pairs or small coveys. Very secretive, preferring to run if disturbed. Flies expertly through trees. Best located by sitting quietly and listening for sounds of feeding birds on leaf litter. Roosts in trees. Nests on the ground.

Rufous-throated Partridge
■ *Arborophila rufogularis* 27cm

DESCRIPTION Little-known bird with distinct head and throat pattern; white half-collar and broad chestnut breast-band, rufous-orange ear-coverts, throat and foreneck; black spots on ear-coverts and neck-sides. Sexes alike. **FOOD** Seeds, berries, green plant matter and invertebrates, including larvae. **VOICE** Mournful double whistle, *wheea-whu*, repeated constantly and on ascending scale. **DISTRIBUTION** Subspecies *A. r. rufogularis* and *A. r. intermedia* found in foothills of Himalayas. **HABITAT & HABITS** Similar to those of the Hill Partridge (opposite) occuring in dense understorey of broadleaved evergreen forest. Little known but said to breed on cushion of grass under rocks in forests.

Blood Pheasant ■ *Ithaginis cruentus* 38cm

DESCRIPTION Medium-sized, red and grey game bird with thick crest. Varies according to race. Male: white-streaked grey above and greyish-white with variable amounts of red below but always on vent and tail. Head and neck variably patterned red and black, with grey or black crest. Red skin around eyes. Female: dark brown with grey nape and crest. Very short-tailed for a pheasant.

FOOD Moss, lichen, leaf litter and grass shoots; beetle wing-cases; other insects. **VOICE** Squealing *kzeeuuk cheeu cheeu chee*; repeated *chuck*. **DISTRIBUTION** Locally common breeding resident in high northern mountains from W Nepal east to Arunachal Pradesh. Moves lower in winter. Also Tibet, Myanmar and China. **HABITAT & HABITS** Inhabits open forest and scrub near snowline. Feeds gregariously on the ground, scratching (often through deep snow) for food. Usually very confiding. Runs strongly and rarely flies. Roosts in trees. Nests on the ground.

Koklass Pheasant ■ *Pucrasia macrolopha* 58–64cm

DESCRIPTION Large, grey and brown game bird with long, backswept crest. Races vary in amount of chestnut on underparts. Male: bottle-green head with brown and golden

crown and crest. Prominent white lower cheeks. Underparts chestnut. Flanks silvery-grey of variable extent. Upperparts similar. Dark, pointed tail. Female: paler with short crest and cheek-spots. **FOOD** Variety of seeds and invertebrates. **VOICE** Noisy. Crowing *khok kok kok kokha* and various chuckles. **DISTRIBUTION** Locally common breeding resident in northern mountains from N Pakistan east to C Nepal. Mover lower down in winter. Also Asia and China. **HABITAT & HABITS** Inhabits montane forested hillsides and ravines. Feeds in pairs on the ground. Very shy, running or flying rapidly when disturbed. Roosts in trees.

Himalayan Monal ■ *Lophophorus impejanus* 70cm

DESCRIPTION Large, brightly coloured game bird with plumed crest. Male: iridescent purple-blue above with chestnut tail and wings. Underparts black, including foreneck and face. Blue, round eye. Rear neck coppery-yellow becoming greener on mantle. White back-

patch. Female: white flecked brown with white throat. **FOOD** Seeds, tubers, shoots, berries and insects. **VOICE** Loud whistle, *whhee uu*, like Eurasian Curlew's (p. 40). **DISTRIBUTION** Locally common breeding resident in northern mountains from N Pakistan east to Arunachal Pradesh. Moves lower down in winter. Also Tibet. **HABITAT & HABITS** Inhabits rocky and grassy slopes at or above treeline, moving down into open forest in winter. Also active cultivation, particularly potatoes. Feeds on the ground, usually in small groups. Digs into the ground, often through snow. More confiding than most game birds.

Satyr Tragopan ■ *Tragopan satyra* 67–72cm

DESCRIPTION Large, brightly coloured game bird with blue face. Male's underparts mainly white-spotted crimson-red. Black and white-spotted brown upperparts with red on wings, and dark brown rump and tail. Blue face surrounded by black extending on to neck-sides. Female white-spotted rufous-brown. **FOOD** Seeds, leaves, grass and root parts, and insect wings; invertebrates.

VOICE Loud, wailing *guwaah guwaah guwaah*, becoming louder and more extended. Also *wak wak* alarm call. **DISTRIBUTION** Scarce and very local breeding resident in northern mountains from Uttaranchal east to Arunachal Pradesh. Common only in Bhutan. Moves lower down in winter. Also Tibet. **HABITAT & HABITS** Inhabits montane forest undergrowth, particularly on slopes and in ravines. Feeds in the open on the ground, in morning and evening. Confiding where unmolested, but tends to keep hidden. Nests in tree.

Red Junglefowl ■ *Gallus gallus* 65–75cm

DESCRIPTION Origin of domestic chickens. Male: golden-brown hackles covering neck and back, golden and green wings, and black underparts; thick, long, curved black tail; white rump; red comb and wattles. Female: speckled reddish-brown, with golden neck and small red comb and wattles. Cocked tail. May be confused with hybrids with domestic fowl. **FOOD** Grain crops, tubers and insects. **VOICE** Shrill, rushed crow, *kuk ku rudi ru*, reminiscent of domestic chicken. Cackling alarm call in flight. **DISTRIBUTION** Locally common breeding resident in northern foothills from Jammu and Kashmir east to Myanmar border and south into north-eastern plains south to Orissa and Madhya Pradesh. Also Bangladesh. Associated with distribution of natural sal forests. Also China and SE Asia. **HABITAT & HABITS** Inhabits well-watered forest and secondary growth. Appears on roads in morning and evening. Feeds in groups, usually with one male, on the ground. Very shy, running rapidly or flying when alarmed. Roosts in trees.

Kalij Pheasant ■ *Lophura leucomelanos* 65cm

DESCRPTION Large, dark game bird with black crest. *Leucomelanos* is similar to race *hamiltoni* but with more muted scaling above and black crest. Can have whitish neck as

shown. *Lathami* is all black with white scaling on rump. Black crest and red face. *Moffitti* is all black with no scaling. Also has black crest and red face. **FOOD** Omnivorous. Bamboo seeds and small snakes, but especially termites, figs, forest yams and bamboo seeds. **VOICE** Loud crowing by male. Chuckling calls on disturbance. **DISTRIBUTION** Locally common breeding resident in northern mountains. *Laucomelanos* occurs in C and E Nepal, *Lathami* in E Himalayas and NE India, and *moffiiti* in C Bhutan. *Lathami* also in Myanmar. **HABITAT & HABITS** Found in forest undergrowth, clearings and terraced cultivation.

Indian Peafowl
■ *Pavo cristatus* 180–230cm

DESCRIPTION Huge, very familiar game bird with tufted crest. Adult male has train of elongated green upper tail-coverts to 1.5m long. Train covered by blue-centred 'eyes'. Fanned high in shimmering display. Small head and long neck deep blue. Grey coverts and chestnut wings. Female brown, whitish below with black-barred foreneck and breast, and green hindneck. **FOOD** Seeds, berries, shoots, tubers, invertebrates and reptiles. **VOICE** Loud, wailing *may yow*. Also cackling. **DISTRIBUTION** India's national bird. Locally common endemic breeding resident throughout lowlands of India, Sri Lanka and Nepal. Most common in north. Large feral populations in northern, western and central areas. Very rare in Pakistan and gone from Bangladesh. Feral in Europe and elsewhere. **HABITAT & HABITS** Inhabits forest undergrowth, and where feral, villages, cultivation and some towns. Feeds methodically on the ground in small parties. Often confiding. Roosts high in trees. Nests on the ground.

Asian Openbill
■ *Anastomus oscitans* 68cm

DESCRIPTION Large, erect, black and white waterbird with long, permanently open bill. Rather stocky. Smoky-grey wash in non-breeding plumage. Glossy black flight feathers and black tail. Bill pinkish-grey and both mandibles curved to leave distinctive 'nutcracker' gap. Legs reddish. Sexes alike. Immature dark brownish-grey. **FOOD** Snails and occasionally other small aquatic animals, such as frogs and crabs. **VOICE** Voiceless. Clatters bill at nest. **DISTRIBUTION** Locally common breeding resident throughout lowlands but rare in Pakistan. Also SE Asia. **HABITAT & HABITS** Inhabits larger wetlands. Rare on coast. Gregarious, nesting in tree colonies, often with other waterbirds. Feeds mainly on molluscs, which it cracks open with its specially adapted bill. Often soars high on thermals. Flies with neck and legs extended.

Lesser Adjutant ■ *Leptoptilos javanicus* 110–120cm

DESCRIPTION Huge, black and white stork, with bare pinkish-orange head and neck, and powerful pink bill. Wings, neck-ruff and mantle blackish; coppery spots on wings in breeding plumage. White underparts and armpits. Slight scruffy black crest on rear crown and black down on rear neck. No neck pouch.

FOOD Fish, especially mudskippers; also frogs, reptiles, crustaceans, locusts, rats, grasshoppers and some carrion. **VOICE** Silent. Clatters bill at nest. **DISTRIBUTION** Globally threatened; now rare but widespread breeding resident throughout lowlands except Pakistan. Most frequent in Nepal and north-east. Wanders outside breeding season. Also rarely China and SE Asia. **HABITAT & HABITS** Inhabits marshes, jheels and mangroves. Usually solitary and very shy. Feeds by walking slowly on the ground or through shallow water to locate prey. Small colonies or individual pairs nest high in forest trees. Characteristic hunched posture with neck withdrawn in flight, like a heron.

Greater Adjutant ■ *Leptoptilos dubius* 120–150cm

DESCRIPTION Huge, grey and white stork with bare pink head, neck and pendulous neck

pouch, and massive pale pink bill. Thick white neck-ruff and white underparts. Dark grey flight feathers and light grey upperwing panel and undertail, differing from the Lesser Adjutant's (p. 19). Head and neck also barer and bill even more powerful. FOOD Carrion, birds, large fish, frogs and crabs. VOICE Silent apart from croaks and bill-clattering. DISTRIBUTION Globally threatened and now very rare except in Assam, where locally common. Could still occur anywhere as it wanders after breeding, but numbers are very small. Also very rarely in SE Asia. HABITAT & HABITS Inhabits marshes, jheels, cultivation and urban rubbish dumps. Formerly renowned scavenger in towns. Usually in small groups, standing motionless or sedately walking over the ground or through water. Nests high in trees alone or in colonies. Posture and flight as Lesser's.

Black Stork
■ *Ciconia nigra* 90–100cm

DESCRIPTION Huge, erect, black and white waterbird with long red bill and legs. All black with green and purple gloss, and white lower breast and belly. White triangles on underwing obvious in overhead flight. Sexes alike. Immature browner than adults, with grey-green bill and legs. Tail sometimes has some white in it. FOOD Fish, frogs, crustaceans, reptiles and insects. VOICE Voiceless. DISTRIBUTION Scarce winter visitor mainly to northern areas. Also Europe, Africa and W, C and E Asia. HABITAT & HABITS Solitary or in small groups. Very wary. Inhabits marshes, jheels and particularly lakes in wooded areas. Feeds in shallow water or waterside grass. Stately, measured walk. Flies with neck and legs extended. Often soars high on thermals.

Painted Stork ■ *Mycteria leucocephala* 95cm

DESCRIPTION Sexes alike. White plumage; blackish-green and white wings; blackish-green breast-band and black tail; rich rosy-pink wash on greater wing-coverts; large, slightly curved, orangish-yellow bill. Young pale dirty brown, with neck feathers edged darker; lack breast-band. **FOOD** Fish, frogs and crustaceans. **VOICE** Characteristic mandible clattering of storks; young in nest have grating begging calls. **DISTRIBUTION** Resident and local migrant, from terai south through area's well-watered regions. **HABITAT & HABITS** Found in inland marshes and jheels; occasionally riversides. Common and gregarious. Feeds with bill partly submerged, ready to grab prey. When not feeding, settles hunched up outside water. Regularly soars high on thermals.

Asian Woollyneck ■ *Ciconia episcopus* 105cm

DESCRIPTION Sexes alike. Large, black and white stork with red legs; glossy black crown, back and breast, and huge wings, with black parts having distinct purplish-green sheen; white neck, lower abdomen and undertail-coverts; long, stout bill black, occasionally tinged crimson. In young birds, glossy black replaced by dark brown. **FOOD** Lizards, frogs and crabs. **VOICE** Only clattering of mandibles. **DISTRIBUTION** Resident in subcontinent, to about 1,400m in Himalayas. **HABITAT & HABITS** Occurs in marshes, cultivation and wet grassland. Solitary or in small scattered parties, feeding with other storks, ibises and egrets. Stalks on dry land, and settles on trees.

Black-headed Ibis ■ *Threskiornis melanocephalus* 75cm

DESCRIPTION Sexes alike. White plumage; naked black head; long, curved black bill; blood-red patches seen on underwing and flanks in flight. Breeding: long plumes over neck;

some slaty-grey in wings. Young: head and neck feathered; only face and patch around eye naked. **FOOD** Frogs, insects, fish, molluscs and algal matter. **VOICE** Loud, booming call. **DISTRIBUTION** Resident; local migrant. Subcontinent, from terai south. **HABITAT & HABITS** Occurs in marshes and on riversides. Gregarious; feeds with storks, spoonbills, egrets and other ibises. Moves actively in water, the long, curved bill held partly open and head partly submerged as it probes nutrient-rich mud.

Red-naped Ibis

■ *Pseudibis papillosa* 70cm

DESCRIPTION Sexes alike. Glossy black plumage; slender, blackish-green, downcurved bill; red warts on naked black head; white shoulder-patch; brick-red legs. The **Glossy Ibis** *Plegadis falcinellus* is deep maroon-brown above, with purple-green gloss from head to lower back; feathered head and lack of white shoulder-patch distinctive. **FOOD** Small fish, frogs, earthworms, insects, lizards and crustaceans. **VOICE** Loud, 2–3-note nasal screams, uttered in flight. **DISTRIBUTION** Resident. NW India, east through Gangetic Plain; south to Karnataka. **HABITAT & HABITS** Occurs in cultivated areas and edges of marshes. Found in small parties. Spends most time on drier edges of marshes and jheels. In shallow water, often feeds with other ibises, storks and spoonbills.

Glossy Ibis

Black Bittern ■ *Ixobrychus flavicollis* 58cm

DESCRIPTION Medium-sized, very dark heron, with bold yellow neck-stripe. Upperparts dull black, browner on female than male. Whitish-streaked rufous and black below. Belly grey. Immature more streaked than adults and upperpart feathers have buff fringes.

FOOD Fish, frogs, lizards, molluscs and crustaceans. **VOICE** Occasional harsh *ker*. Male's breeding call a deep boom like a distant foghorn. **DISTRIBUTION** Scarce breeding resident throughout. Most frequent in north-east, Sri Lanka and extreme south-west. Appears to be mainly a monsoon breeding visitor to north-west. Also China and SE Asia. **HABITAT & HABITS** Inhabits reed beds with bushes, and bushy margins of canals, rivers and jheels. Crepuscular, solitary and very secretive. May fly quite high to feeding sites. Often hunts from bushes, sitting motionless for hours waiting for prey. Usually nests low in waterside bush.

Oriental Darter ■ *Anhinga melanogaster* 90cm

DESCRIPTION Sexes alike. Long, snake-like neck, pointed bill and stiff, fan-shaped tail confirm identity. Adult: black above, streaked and mottled with silvery-grey on back and wings; chocolate-brown head and neck; white stripe down sides of upper neck; white chin and upper throat; entirely black below. Young: brown with rufous and silvery streaks on mantle. **FOOD** Mostly fish. **VOICE** Loud croaks and squeaks. **DISTRIBUTION** Subcontinent, south of Himalayan foothills. **HABITAT & HABITS** Inhabits freshwater lakes and jheels. Bird of deep, fresh water; small numbers scattered along with Little Cormorants (p. 24). Highly specialized feeder – entire structure modified for following and capturing fish underwater. Swims low in water with only head and neck uncovered. Chases prey below water with wings half open, spearing it with sudden, rapier-like thrusts made possible by bend in neck at eighth and ninth vertebrae, which acts as a spring as it straightens. Tosses fish into air and swallows it head-first. Basks on tree stumps and rocks, cormorant style.

Great Cormorant ■ *Phalacrocorax carbo* 80cm

DESCRIPTION Sexes alike. Breeding adult: black plumage with metallic blue-green sheen; white facial skin and throat; bright yellow gular pouch and white thigh-patches;

silky white plumes on head and neck. Non-breeding adult: no white thigh-patches; gular pouch less bright. First year young: dull brown above, white below. **FOOD** Fish. **VOICE** Usually slient. **DISTRIBUTION** Resident in most areas; subcontinent, to 3,000m in Himalayas. **HABITAT & HABITS** Occurs in jheels, lakes, mountain torrents and occasionally coastal lagoons. Aquatic. Not a gregarious species outside breeding season. Usually one or two birds feeding close by. Dives underwater in search of fish.

Little Cormorant
■ *Microcarbo niger* 50cm

DESCRIPTION Sexes alike. India's smallest and most common cormorant. Short, thick neck and head distinctive; lacks gular patch. The **Indian Cormorant** *P. fuscicollis* is larger, with a more oval-shaped head. Breeding adult: black plumage has blue-green sheen; silky white feathers on forecrown and sides of head; silvery-grey wash on upper back and wing-coverts, speckled with black. Non-breeding adult: white chin and upper throat. **FOOD** Mainly fish; also tadpoles and crustaceans. **VOICE** Mostly slient. **DISTRIBUTION** Subcontinent, south of Himalayas. **HABITAT & HABITS** Occurs in village tanks, jheels, lakes, and occasionally rivers and coastal areas. Gregarious; flocks in large jheels. Swims with only head and short neck exposed, diving often; the hunt can become a noisy, jostling scene. Frequently perches on poles, trees and rocks, and basks with wings spread open.

Oriental Honey-buzzard ■ *Pernis ptilorhynchus* 67cm

DESCRIPTION Sexes alike. Slender head and longish neck distinctive; tail rarely fanned.
Highly variable phases. Mostly darkish brown above; crest rarely visible; pale brown underbody, with narrow whitish bars; pale underside of wings barred; broad, dark subterminal tail-band; 2–3 more bands on tail; tarsus unfeathered. **FOOD** Bee larvae, honey, small birds and lizards; occasionally robs poultry. **VOICE** High-pitched, long-drawn *weeeeeu…* **DISTRIBUTION** Resident and local migrant; subcontinent to about 2,000m in Himalayas. **HABITAT & HABITS** Occurs in forest, open country, cultivation and vicinity of villages. Solitary or in pairs, perching on forest trees or flying. Often enters villages and outskirts of small towns.

Black-winged Kite
■ *Elanus caeruleus* 32cm

DESCRIPTION Sexes alike. Pale grey-white plumage, whiter on head, neck and underbody; short black stripe through eye; black shoulder-patches and wing-tips distinctive at rest and in flight; blood-red eyes. Young: upper body tinged brown, with pale edges to feathers. **FOOD** Insects, lizards, rodents and snakes. **VOICE** High-pitched squeal. **DISTRIBUTION** Subcontinent, to about 1,500m in outer Himalayas. **HABITAT & HABITS** Found in open scrub and grass country; also light forest. Usually solitary or in pairs. Rests on exposed perch or flies over open scrub and grass country. Mostly hunts on the wing, regularly hovering like a kestrel to scan the ground; drops height to check when hovering, with legs held ready.

Black Kite ■ *Milvus migrans* 60cm

DESCRIPTION Sexes alike. Dark brown plumage; forked tail, easily seen in flight; underparts faintly streaked. The **Black-eared Kite** M. *m. lineatus*, breeding in Himalayas and wintering in C India, is slightly larger, with conspicuous white patch on underwing, visible in overhead flight. **FOOD** Omnivorous, feeding on refuse, dead rats, earthworms, insects, nestlings of smaller birds and poultry. **VOICE** Loud, musical whistle. **DISTRIBUTION** Resident; subcontinent to about 2,200m in Himalayas, co-existing with the Black-eared in some localities. **HABITAT & HABITS** Mostly found in neighbourhood of humans. Common and gregarious; most common near humans, thriving on refuse generated by them, often in the most crowded localities. Roosts communally.

Black-eared Kite

Brahminy Kite ■ *Haliastur indus* 80cm

DESCRIPTION Sexes alike. White head, neck, upper back and breast; rest of plumage rich and rusty-chestnut; brownish abdomen and darker tips to flight feathers visible mostly in flight. Young: brown, like the Black Kite (above) but with rounded tail. **FOOD** Mostly stranded fish; also frogs, insects, lizards, mudskippers, small snakes and rodents. **VOICE** Loud scream. **DISTRIBUTION** Resident and local migrant; subcontinent, to about 1,800m in Himalayas. **HABITAT & HABITS** Found in margins of lakes, marshes, rivers and sea coasts. Solitary or in small, scattered parties. Loves water, and frequently scavenges near lakes and marshes, and around villages and towns.

Juvenile

Egyptian Vulture ■ *Neophron percnopterus* 65cm

DESCRIPTION Sexes alike. White plumage; blackish in wings; naked yellow head, neck and throat; yellow bill; thick ruff of feathers around neck; wedge-shaped tail and blackish flight feathers distinctive in overhead flight. Nominate race of NW India slightly larger, with dark, horny bill. **FOOD** Refuse, carrion, insects and stranded turtles; particularly adept at opening live turtles. **VOICE** Usually silent. **DISTRIBUTION** All India; plains to about 2,000m in Himalayas. **HABITAT & HABITS** Found in open country, in vicinity of human habitation. Several usually occur together, perched on top of ruins or earthen mounds, or just walking on the ground. Glides a lot but rarely soars high. Sometimes with other vultures.

Juvenile

White-rumped Vulture
■ *Gyps bengalensis* 90cm

DESCRIPTION Sexes alike. Blackish-brown plumage; almost naked head has whitish ruff around base. White rump (lower back) distinctive, when perched and often in flight. In overhead flight, white underwing-coverts contrast with dark underbody and flight feathers. Young birds brown with no white on underwing in flight. **FOOD** Mostly scavenges on carcasses. **VOICE** Loud screeches when feeding. **DISTRIBUTION** Resident; all India, to about 2,800m in Himalayas. **HABITAT & HABITS** Found in open country. Increasingly uncommon, and now rarely seen at carcasses, slaughter houses and refuse dumps. When resting, head and neck are dug into shoulders. Soars high on thermals. Several converge on a carcass. Basks in the sun.

Red-headed Vulture
■ *Sarcogyps calvus* 85cm

DESCRIPTION Sexes alike. Black plumage with white on thighs and breast; naked red head, neck and feet. In overhead flight, white breast, thigh-patches and grey-white band along wings are distinctive. Widely spread primaries. Young birds darkish-brown with white abdomen and undertail. **FOOD** Mainly scavenges on carcasses. **VOICE** Hoarse croak. **DISTRIBUTION** Resident; all India, to about 2,800m in Himalayas; uncommon. **HABITAT & HABITS** Found in open country and village outskirts. Mostly solitary but 2–4 individuals may be seen at a carcass with other vultures; usually does not mix with the rest.

Crested Serpent Eagle ■ *Spilornis cheela* 75cm

DESCRIPTION Sexes alike; female larger than male. Dark brown plumage; roundish, pied crest, visible when erected; pale brown below, finely spotted white. In overhead flight, dark

body, white bars along wings and white tail-band confirm identity. **FOOD** Snakes, lizards, birds and rodents, including squirrels. **VOICE** Characteristic call. Loud, whistling scream, *keee…kee…ke…* **DISTRIBUTION** Resident; subcontinent, to about 3,000m in Himalayas. **HABITAT & HABITS** Found in forested country. Solitary or in pairs, flying over forest, often very high, and calling frequently. Perches on leafy branches. Swoops down on prey, snatching it in its talons. Raises crest when alarmed.

Juvenile

Western Marsh Harrier ■ *Circus aeruginosus* 55cm

DESCRIPTION Male: dark brown plumage; dull rufous head and breast; silvery-grey wings and tail; black wing-tips (best seen in flight). Female (and young): chocolate-brown; buff on head and shoulders; like the Black Kite (p. 26), but tail rounded (not forked). **FOOD** Fish, rodents, frogs, small waterbirds and insects. **VOICE** Usually silent. **DISTRIBUTION** Common winter visitor; subcontinent, south of foothills country. Most common in India. **HABITAT & HABITS** Occurs in marshes, jheels and wet cultivation. Solitary or in pairs. Sails low over a marsh, grassland or cultivation. Often drops to the ground, frequently vanishing in dense grass and reed growth. Perches on mounds or edges of marshes.

Shikra ■ *Accipiter badius* 32cm

DESCRIPTION Ashy-grey above; whitish below, close-barred with rust-brown; grey throat-stripe. In flight, multi-banded tail and roundish wings help identification; golden-yellow eyes and yellow legs and feet seen at close range. Migrant **Eurasian Sparrowhawk** A. *nisus* very similar, but a closer look reveals longer legs, rufous cheek-patch and absence of mesial stripe in *nisus*. **FOOD** Rodents, small birds, lizards and large insects; also robs poultry. **VOICE** Loud, drongo-like *titew…titew*. **DISTRIBUTION** Resident; subcontinent, to 1,600m in Himalayas. **HABITAT & HABITS** Occurs in light forest, open country and neighbourhoods of villages; also cities. Usually solitary. Hides in leafy branches. Pounces on unsuspecting prey; occasionally chases small birds. Soars over forest.

White-eyed Buzzard
■ *Butastur teesa* 45cm

DESCRIPTION Sexes alike. Ashy-brown above; distinct throat, white with two dark cheek-stripes and third stripe from chin; white nape-patch, white eyes and orange-yellow cere visible at close quarters. In flight, pale shoulder-patch seen from above; from below, pale underside of roundish wings against darkish body distinctive. **FOOD** Rodents, including squirrels, lizards, small birds, frogs and insects. **VOICE** Musical, plaintive *te...twee*, frequently when breeding. **DISTRIBUTION** Resident; subcontinent, to about 1,200m in Himalayas. **HABITAT & HABITS** Occurs in open and dry forests, and cultivated country. Solitary or in scattered pairs. Seen on exposed perches, trees, poles and telegraph wires. Seems to prefer certain sites. Soars high and does aerial displays when breeding.

Greater Spotted Eagle ■ *Clanga clanga* 65cm

DESCRIPTION Sexes alike, but female slightly larger than male. Deep brown above, with purplish wash on back; somewhat paler below; often has whitish rump. Soars on

straight wings, with drooping tips. Immature birds may have white markings above. The **Indian Spotted Eagle** *C. hastata* is slightly smaller, with narrower wings, and paler above. **FOOD** Small animals, including waterfowl and small birds. **VOICE** Loud, shrill *kaek...kaek...*, often from perch. **DISTRIBUTION** Breeds sporadically in parts of N, E and NC India; spreads south in winter. **HABITAT & HABITS** Found in tree-covered areas near water. Mostly solitary. Prefers vicinity of water. Perches for long spells on bare trees or on the ground. Sluggish behaviour.

Changeable Hawk Eagle ▪ *Nisaetus (cirrhatus) limnaeetus* 63–77m

DESCRIPTION Sexes alike, but female larger than male. Large, slender, crested forest eagle. Brown above; white underbody longitudinally streaked all over with brown; prominent occipital crest. Streaked whitish body, broad wings and long, rounded tail distinctive in flight. The **Changeable Hawk Eagle** *N. c. limnaeetus*, of Himalayan foothills and NE India very similar, except for smaller, often indistinct crest. **FOOD** Partridges, other ground birds, squirrels, hares and lizards. **VOICE** Loud, screaming cry, usually long drawn. **DISTRIBUTION** Resident; subcontinent, south of Himalayas. **HABITAT & HABITS** Occupies semi-evergreen and deciduous forests and clearings. Solitary; occasionally a pair circles high over forests, especially when breeding. Surveys for prey from high, leafy branches near forest clearings.

Steppe Eagle ▪ *Aquila nipalensis* 76–80cm

DESCRIPTION Large, dark eagle with dark irises. Larger and more fierce looking than the **Tawny Eagle** *A. rapax*, but very similar to dark phases. Adults dark brown, barred on flight feathers and tail, and often with yellowish nape-patch. Always has pale throat. Immature paler with broad white underwing-bars, trailing edges, tail-tip and rump-crescent. Gape extends to rear of eye. Thick-feathered legs and oval nostrils. **FOOD** Birds, eggs, lizards, small mammals, frogs, bats and large insects. **VOICE** Usually silent. **DISTRIBUTION** Fairly common winter visitor mainly to northern lowlands. Scarcer further south. Also E Europe, Africa, and W, C and E Asia. **HABITAT & HABITS** Inhabits all types of lightly wooded and open country, with a preference for wetlands, unlike Tawny. Pirates animal prey from other raptors and also eats carrion, including fish. Soars on flat wings, often with tips raised and fingers spread.

Booted Eagle ■ *Hieraaetus pennatus* 45–53cm

DESCRIPTION Medium-sized (smallest eagle), stocky raptor with square-cut, long tail and two colour phases. Dark phase dark brown with distinct, pale wedge on inner primaries, pale upperwing patches and small white 'landing lights' at wing junctions. May be confused

with square-tailed Black Kite (p. 26). Pale phase streaked, rather creamy-brown and buffish-white below. Wing markings are the same. Sexes similar. Soars with flat wings. **FOOD** Small birds, rodents and lizards; robs poultry. **VOICE** Noisy when breeding. Rapid *kwe kwe*. **DISTRIBUTION** Fairly common winter visitor throughout lowlands. Scarce in north-east. Nepal. Bangladesh and Sri Lanka. Breeds in northern mountains and occasionally in peninsula. Also S Europe, Africa, and W and C Asia. **HABITAT & HABITS** Inhabits wooded and open country, including cultivation. Locates animal prey from soaring flight, then pounces on it in a spectacular dive. Pairs often hunt in unison. Nests in tall trees.

Bonelli's Eagle ■ *Aquila fasciata* 65–72cm

DESCRIPTION Fairly large raptor with long wings and tail and protruding neck. Adults dark brown with streaked white underparts, pale mantle and dark-ended grey

tail. Underwings show contrasting blackish coverts. Immature gingery-brown below with barred tail and pale rump-crescent. Long, feathered legs. Strong, dark-tipped, pale bill. **FOOD** Hares, large ground birds and monitor lizards; also small forest birds and squirrels. **VOICE** High *kee kee kee* when breeding. **DISTRIBUTION** Scarce breeding resident in most of lowlands; very rare in north-east, Bangladesh and Sri Lanka. Wanders in winter. Also S Europe, Africa, and W, C and E Asia. **HABITAT & HABITS** Inhabits well-wooded country, particularly near water. Fierce hunter of medium-sized birds, mammals and reptiles, often pursuing prey in pairs on regular beat. Robs nesting waterbirds of fish. Soars much less than other eagles, preferring to stay close to prey sources. Nests high in large tree.

Mountain Hawk Eagle ■ *Nisaetus nipalensis* 72cm

DESCRIPTION Large, crested forest raptor with well-barred underparts. Not always easily separable from the Changeable Hawk Eagle (p. 31), but less variable, tail shorter and more prominently barred. Belly heavily barred, not streaked. Wing shape different with distinct bulge to secondaries. Southern race has rufous barring below. Immature pale buff below with well-streaked head. Always has long crest, though this is often laid flat. **FOOD** Lizards, small mammals, frogs, bats and large insects. **VOICE** In breeding season, high, whistling *peeo peeo*. **DISTRIBUTION** Locally common breeding resident in northern mountains, Western Ghats and Sri Lanka. Also Myanmar, China and Japan. **HABITAT & HABITS** Inhabits upland forests. Frequently soars over canopy, often in pairs, but otherwise behaves as Changeable.

Golden Eagle ■ *Aquila chrysaetos* 75–88cm

DESCRIPTION Huge raptor with broad, long wings, long tail, and protruding head and neck. Adults brown with paler coverts, golden crown and nape. Tail-tip darker. Immature has different amounts of white but, most typically, broad white wing-flashes and tail-base. Heavily feathered legs. Flies with wings in pronounced 'V', with wing-tips raised. Trailing edges markedly curved. **FOOD** Mammals, mainly rodents and hares; also birds, particularly game birds, lizards and snakes, as well as carrion. **VOICE** Usually silent. **DISTRIBUTION** Scarce breeding resident of northern mountains, rarely wandering to plains in winter. Also Europe, Africa, W and E Asia, and America. **HABITAT & HABITS** Inhabits mountains above treeline and near steep cliffs, and open country in plains. Usually solitary or in pairs. Very powerful hunter, locating animal prey in soaring flight and pursuing it close to the ground. Nests on cliff ledge or tree.

Oriental Hobby ■ *Falco severus* 28cm

DESCRIPTION Sexes alike. Small, robust falcon; slaty-grey above; deep black head, including cheeks; chestnut underparts, paler on throat. The **Eurasian Hobby** F. *subbuteo* has rusty-white underparts, thickly streaked. **FOOD** Large flying insects, small bats, birds and lizards. **VOICE** Shrill trill of 3–4 notes.

Above: *Eurasian Hobby*

DISTRIBUTION Resident in Himalayas and NE India. **HABITAT & HABITS** Occurs in forested, hilly country. Solitary or several together. Feeds mostly around dusk and dawn, in twilight. Flies about erratically, circling, dancing, rising and dropping. Charges after prey at tremendous speed. Eats on the wing or on a perch.

Common Kestrel ■ *Falco tinnunculus* 35cm

DESCRIPTION Male: black-streaked, ash-grey crown, sides of neck and nape; rufous mantle, black spotted; cheek-stripe; grey tail has white tip and black subterminal band; streaked and spotted buffy underbody. Female: pale rufous above; streaked head and narrowly barred back; paler buff below, densely streaked. Young: like female; thickly streaked below. **FOOD** Insects, lizards and small rodents. **VOICE** Infrequent clicking sound. **DISTRIBUTION** Resident and local migrant; several races. Breeds in Himalayas (most common in west); also Western Ghats south of Mumbai; associated hill ranges in S India; winter numbers augmented. **HABITAT & HABITS** Found in open country and cliffsides. Solitary or in pairs. Occurs on exposed perches overlooking open country. Circles in air and pounces into grass and scrub; often hovers when hunting.

Sarus Crane ■ *Antigone antigone* 165cm

DESCRIPTION Sexes alike, but female slightly smaller than male; grey plumage; naked red head and upper neck. Young birds brownish-grey, with rusty-brown on head. **FOOD** Fish, frogs, crustaceans, insects, grains and tubers. **VOICE** Very loud, far-reaching trumpeting, often duet between pair. Elaborate dancing rituals. **DISTRIBUTION** Most common in C India (E Rajasthan, Gujarat, and C Madhya Pradesh, Gangetic Plain). **HABITAT & HABITS** Found in marshes, jheels, well-watered cultivation and village ponds. Occurs in pairs, family parties or flocks; also feeds with other waterbirds. Pairs for life and usually well protected in N and W-C India, but habitat loss continues to be a grave threat. Flies under 12m off the ground.

Demoiselle Crane ■ *Grus virgo* 75cm

DESCRIPTION Sexes alike. Overall plumage grey; black head and neck; prominent white ear-tufts; long black feathers of lower neck fall over breast; brownish-grey secondaries sickle shaped and drooping over tail. Young birds have grey head and much shorter drooping secondaries over tail than adults. **FOOD** Wheat, paddy and gram; does extensive damage to winter crops. **VOICE** High-pitched, sonorous *kraak… kraak…* calls. **DISTRIBUTION** Winter visitor; most common in NW India and over E Rajasthan, Gujarat and Madhya Pradesh, and sporadic over much of area. **HABITAT & HABITS** Found in winter crop fields, sandy riverbanks, ponds and jheel edges. Occurs in huge flocks in winter, often numbering many thousands. Feeds in early mornings and early evenings in cultivation; rests during hot hours on marsh edges and sandbanks. Flies en masse when disturbed.

Black-necked Crane ■ *Grus nigricollis* 139cm

DESCRIPTION Large grey crane with black head and neck, and black, drooping tertials. Flight feathers black. Crown red, legs blackish, bill grey. Sexes alike. Immature rusty-brown. **FOOD** Plant roots and tubers, grains, snails, fish, shrimps, frogs, lizards, small birds, pikas and large insects. **VOICE** Loud, rather high-pitched *ker kra krew*. **DISTRIBUTION** Globally endangered endemic breeding resident that breeds in small numbers in Himalayas and winters mainly in Bhutan. **HABITAT & HABITS** Breeds by high-altitude lakes and winters on wet fallow, stubble and marshes. Often very tame as revered by Buddhists. Nests on lake islands.

Bengal Florican ■ *Houbaropsis bengalensis* 66cm

DESCRIPTION Large, stocky bustard with black head, neck and underparts. Almost completely white wings. Back warm brown with black feather-tips. Larger female and first-year male buff on head, neck and breast, and white on belly. Crown black with buff central

stripe. Wings buff. Yellow irises. **FOOD** Shoots, flowers, grasses, seeds and berries, but also insects such as locusts, grasshoppers, beetles, ants, and occasionally lizards. **VOICE** Clicking sound in display and when flushed. **DISTRIBUTION** Globally threatened breeding resident now restricted to a few sites in terai and Assam. Also Cambodia. **HABITAT & HABITS** Inhabits wet grassland. Most obvious in breeding season when males leap above grassland in exuberant display. Ventures into short grass and burnt-over areas at beginning and end of day. Usually solitary but males do gather at leks. Nests on the ground.

River Lapwing ▪ *Vanellus duvaucelii* 30cm

DESCRIPTION Sexes alike. Black forehead, crown, and crest drooping over back; sandy grey-brown above; black and white wings; black chin and throat, bordered white; grey-brown breast-band; white below with black patch on belly; black spur at bend of wing. **FOOD** Crustaceans, insects and small frogs. **VOICE** Rather like that of the **Red-wattled Lapwing** V. *indicus*, only a bit softer and less shrill; also sharp *deed…did…did…* **DISTRIBUTION** Breeds in parts of E and C India, including Orissa, Andhra Pradesh and E Madhya Pradesh; may disperse in winter. **HABITAT & HABITS** Usually pairs in close vicinity of stony river beds and sandbanks; sometimes collects around jheels in winter. May collect into small parties during winter, sometimes with other waders. Makes short dashes or feeds at water's edge. Often remains in hunched posture, when not easy to spot; slow flight. Often swims and dives.

Yellow-wattled Lapwing ▪ *Vanellus malabaricus* 28cm

DESCRIPTION Sexes alike. Jet-black cap, bordered with white; sandy-brown upper body; black band in white tail; in flight, white bar in black wings; black chin and throat; sandy-brown breast; black band on lower breast; white below; yellow lappets above and in front of eyes and yellow legs diagnostic. **FOOD** Mostly insects. **VOICE** Short, plaintive notes; on the whole a quiet bird; quick-repeated notes when nest site intruded upon. **DISTRIBUTION** From NW India south throughout area; does not occur in extreme north-east. **HABITAT & HABITS** Found in dry, open country. Solitary or in pairs; rarely in small gatherings; sometimes with more common **Red-wattled Lapwing** V. *indicus*. Quiet and unobtrusive. Feeds on the ground, moving suspiciously.

Red-wattled Lapwing

Little Ringed Plover ■ *Charadrius dubius* 16cm

DESCRIPTION Sexes alike. Sandy-brown above; white forehead; black bands on head and breast and white neck-ring diagnostic; white chin and throat; lack of wing-bar in flight and yellow legs and ring around eye additional clues to identity. **FOOD** Insects, worms

and tiny crabs. **VOICE** *Few…few…* whistle, high-pitched but somewhat plaintive, uttered mostly on the wing. **DISTRIBUTION** Resident and local migrant; throughout area south from Himalayan foothills. **HABITAT & HABITS** Found on shingle-covered riverbanks, tidal mudflats, estuaries and lake edges, in small numbers, often with other shorebirds. Runs on the ground, on mud and drying jheels. Walks with characteristic bobbing gait, picking food from the ground. On close approach, flies rapidly, low over the ground. Zigzag flight accompanied by whistling note.

Pacific Golden Plover ■ *Pluvialis fulva* 25cm

DESCRIPTION Medium-sized to large shorebird, with short neck and fairly long grey legs. Overall golden-brown, speckled back. Dark head and ear-coverts. Non-breeding adult: buff head, neck and breast streaked darker. Breeding adult: black face, neck, breast and belly; creamy-white forehead and supercilium. Juvenile: similar to non-breeding adult, but with light barring on chest-sides and flanks, and more distinct yellow edges and spots on feathers of crown, back and wings. **FOOD** Mainly insects, molluscs, worms, crustaceans and spiders. **VOICE** Distinct *tu…leep* like that of the **Spotted Redshank** *T. erythropus*, but softer.

DISTRIBUTION Locally common winter visitor to all coasts and inland in Bangladesh and NE

Non-breeding

India. Most common in SE India and Bangaldesh. Scarce but regular passage migrant to inland and elsewhere. **HABITAT** Coastal mudflats; salt pans and grassland. Inland on marshes and jheels.

Greater Painted-snipe ■ *Rostratula benghalensis* 25cm

DESCRIPTION Polyandrous. Breeding female: metallic-olive above, thickly marked buff and black; buff stripe down crown-centre; chestnut throat, breast and neck-sides; white below breast. Breeding male: duller overall; lacks chestnut. Sexes difficult to distinguish when not in breeding plumage. **FOOD** Insects, crustaceans, molluscs and vegetable matter. **VOICE** Common call a long-drawn, mellow note similar to noise made by blowing into bottle mouth. **DISTRIBUTION** Resident throughout area to about 2,000m in Himalayas. **HABITAT & HABITS** Occurs in wet mud and marshes, in areas with a mix of open water and heavy low cover. Crepuscular and nocturnal. Solitary or a few scattered birds. Feeds in squelchy mud but also moves on drier ground. Runs on landing.

Common Snipe ■ *Gallinago gallinago* 28cm

DESCRIPTION Sexes alike. Cryptic-coloured marsh bird; brownish-buff, heavily streaked and marked buff, rufous and black; dull white below. Fast, erratic flight; 14 or 16 tail feathers; whitish wing-lining distinctive, but not easily seen. The **Pintail Snipe** G. *stenura* very similar, but usually distinguished only when held in the hand and with considerable experience. **FOOD** Small molluscs, worms and insects. **VOICE** Loud call when flushed. **DISTRIBUTION** Breeds in parts of W Himalaya; mostly winter visitor over subcontinent, most common in C India. **HABITAT & HABITS** Found in marshland, paddy cultivation and jheel edges. Usually several in dense marsh growth. Very difficult to see unless flushed. Probes with long bill in mud, often in shallow water. Feeds mostly in mornings and evenings, often continuing throughout the night.

Pintail Snipe

Black-tailed Godwit
■ *Limosa limosa* 40cm

DESCRIPTION Sexes alike. Female slightly larger than male. Grey-brown above; whitish below; very long, straight bill; in flight, broad white wing-bars, white rump and black tail-tip distinctive. In summer, dull rufous-red on head, neck and breast, with close-barred lower breast and flanks. **FOOD** Crustaceans, worms, molluscs and aquatic insects. **VOICE** Occasional, fairly loud *kwika…kwik*. **DISTRIBUTION** Winter visitor, fairly common over India; lesser numbers towards E and S India. Bar-tailed most common along western seaboard, south to between Goa and Mumbai. **HABITAT & HABITS** Found in marshes, estuaries and creeks. Gregarious, often with other large waders. Quite active, probing with long bill. Wades in water, with long legs often barely visible. Fast and graceful, low flight.

Non-breeding

Eurasian Curlew ■ *Numenius arquata* 58cm

DESCRIPTION Sexes alike. Large wader. Sandy-brown upper body, scalloped fulvous and black; white rump and lower back; whitish below, streaked black; very long, downcurved bill. Very similar **Whimbrel** *N. phaeopus* smaller, with blackish crown with white stripe through centre, and white stripes on head-sides. **FOOD** Crustaceans, insects and mudskippers. **VOICE** Famed scream; wild, rather musical *cour…leeor cooodee…*, the first note longer. **DISTRIBUTION** Winter visitor; sea coasts, west to east. **HABITAT & HABITS** Found in estuaries, creeks, rivers and large, remote marshes. Mostly solitary. Feeds with other large waders. Runs on the ground, between tidemarks, occasionally venturing into very shallow water. A truly wild and wary bird, not easy to approach.

Common Redshank

■ *Tringa totanus* 28cm

DESCRIPTION Sexes alike. Grey-brown above; whitish below, faintly marked about breast; white rump; broad band along trailing edge of wings; orange-red legs and bill-base. In summer, browner above, marked black and fulvous, and more heavily streaked below. The **Spotted Redshank** *T. erythropus* very similar, but has red at base of only lower mandible. **FOOD** Aquatic insects, crustaceans and molluscs. **VOICE** Quite musical, fairly loud and shrill *tleu…ewh… ewh*, mostly in flight; very similar to Common Greenshank's (below) call, but more shrill and high pitched. **DISTRIBUTION** Breeds in Kashmir, Ladakh; winter visitor all over India; fairly common. **HABITAT & HABITS** Found in marshes, creeks and estuaries. Occurs in small flocks, often with other waders. Makes short dashes, probing and jabbing deep in mud. May also enter water, with long legs completely submerged. Rather alert and suspicious bird.

Spotted Redshank (in breeding plumage)

Common Greenshank

■ *Tringa nebularia* 36cm

DESCRIPTION Sexes alike. Grey-brown above; long, slightly upcurved, blackish bill; white forehead and underbody. In flight, white lower back, rump and absence of white in wings diagnostic. Long greenish legs. In summer, darker above, with blackish centres to feathers. The **Marsh Sandpiper** *T. stagnatilis* very similar, but smaller and with distinctly longer legs and distinctive call. **FOOD** Crustaceans, molluscs and aquatic insects. **VOICE** Wild, ringing *tew…tew…tew…* **DISTRIBUTION** Winter visitor, fairly common in most of area. **HABITAT & HABITS** Found in marshes, estuaries and creeks. Solitary or in small groups of 2–6 birds, often with Common Redshanks (above) and other waders. Feeds at edge of water but may enter water to belly level.

Breeding

Wood Sandpiper ■ *Tringa glareola* 20cm

DESCRIPTION Sexes alike. Grey-brown above, closely spotted with white; slender build; white rump and tail; white below; brown on breast; no wing-bar. Summer: dark olive-brown above, spotted white. The **Green Sandpiper** *T. ochropus* stouter, shier, much darker and glossy brown-olive above; in flight, white rump contrasts strikingly with dark upper body; blackish below wings diagnostic. **FOOD** Crustaceans, insects and molluscs. **VOICE** Quite noisy; sharp, trilling notes on the ground; shrill, somewhat metallic *chiff…chiff* calls when flushed; sometimes loud, sharp *tluie…* call. Green utters distinct, wild, ringing calls when flushed. **DISTRIBUTION** Winter visitor to most of area. **HABITAT & HABITS** Found in wet cultivation, marshes, tidal creeks and mudflats. Occurs in small to medium-size flocks, often with other waders. Quite active, probing deep into mud or feeding at edge.

Common Sandpiper ■ *Actitis hypoleucos* 20cm

DESCRIPTION Sexes alike. Olive-brown above, more ash-brown and streaked brown on head and neck-sides; brown rump; white below; lightly streaked brown on breast. In flight, narrow white wing-bar and brown rump; white 'hook' at shoulder; in summer, darker above and speckled. **FOOD** Crustaceans, insects and molluscs. **VOICE** Shrill *twee…tse…tse…*

tse… note, usually when flushed; longish trilling song. **DISTRIBUTION** Breeds in Himalayas, Kashmir to Uttarakhand to about 3,000m; winter visitor all over area. **HABITAT & HABITS** Found in freshwater marshes, lakes, tidal areas and creeks. One to three birds, either by themselves or scattered amid mixed wader flocks. Quite active; makes short dashes, bobbing and wagging short tail. Usually flies low over water, the rapid wingbeats interspersed with short glides ('vibrating flight') helping in identification.

Black-winged Stilt ■ *Himantopus himantopus* 25cm

DESCRIPTION Male: jet-black mantle and pointed wings; rest of plumage glossy white. Female: dark brown where male is black; black wing underside; black spots on head; duller overall in winter. Very long, pink-red legs diagnostic; extends much beyond tail in flight. **FOOD** Aquatic insects, molluscs and vegetable matter. **VOICE** Shrill notes in flight, very tern-like; noisy when breeding. **DISTRIBUTION** Resident and local migrant over most of area, south from about 1,800m in W Himalayas. **HABITAT & HABITS** Found in marshes, salt pans, tidal creeks and village ponds; also riversides. Gregarious; occurs in large numbers, often with other waders in wetlands. Long legs enable it to enter relatively deep water. Clumsy walk. Submerges head when feeding. Characteristic flight silhouette.

Pied Avocet ■ *Recurvirostra avosetta* 45cm

DESCRIPTION Sexes alike. Black and white plumage, long, bluish legs, and long, slender, upcurved bill diagnostic. In flight, long legs extend much beyond tail. **FOOD** Aquatic insects, minute molluscs and crustaceans. **VOICE** Loud, somewhat fluty *klooeet* or *kloeep* call, mostly on the wing; also some harsh, screaming notes. **DISTRIBUTION** Breeds in Kutch, Balochistan; winter visitor, sporadically over most parts of area, and most common in north-west regions. **HABITAT & HABITS** Found in freshwater marshes, coastal tidal areas and creeks. Usually gregarious; sometimes only 2–3 birds scattered over waterbody. Often enters shallow water. Characteristic sideways movement of head when feeding, with head bent low as upcurved bill sweeps along bottom mud. Also swims and up-ends, duck-like.

Indian Courser ■ *Cursorius coromandelicus* 26cm

DESCRIPTION Sexes alike. Bright rufous crown; white and black stripes above and through eyes to nape; sandy-brown above; chestnut throat and breast and black belly; long whitish legs; in flight, dark underwings. **FOOD** Black beetles and other insects. **VOICE** Soft, hen-like clucking call in flight, when flushed. **DISTRIBUTION** Most of area south of Himalayas, but distribution rather patchy; absent in north-east. **HABITAT & HABITS** Found in open scrub, fallow land and dry cultivation. Occurs in small parties in open country. Strictly a ground bird. Runs in short spurts and feeds on the ground, like plovers, suddenly dipping body when disturbed. Flies strongly for short distance and lands; can fly very high.

Little Pratincole ■ *Glareola lactea* 18cm

DESCRIPTION Sexes alike. Brown forehead; sandy-grey above; during breeding has black stripe from eye to bill; white, squarish tail, tipped black; smoky-brown underbody has rufous wash; whiter on lower breast and abdomen; long, narrow wings and short legs. The **Collared Pratincole** G. *pratincola* larger, with forked tail and black loop on throat. **FOOD** Insects taken on the wing. **VOICE** Soft but harsh call notes in flight. **DISTRIBUTION** Resident and local migrant; subcontinent south of outer Himalayas, from about 1,800m. **HABITAT & HABITS** Found in large and quiet riversides, sandbars, marshy expanses, coastal swamps and tidal creeks. Gregarious; large flocks occur over open expanses, close to water. Very swallow-like in demeanour. Strong, graceful flight over water's surface, catching insects on the wing. Flies high in late evening.

ABOVE: *Collared Pratincole*

Indian Skimmer ■ *Rynchops albicollis* 40cm

DESCRIPTION Sexes alike, but female slightly smaller than male. Slender, pointed winged and tern-like pied plumage, blackish-brown above, contrasting with white underbody; white forehead, neck-collar and wing-bar; diagnostic yellowish-orange bill, with much longer lower mandible; red legs. **FOOD** Mainly fish. **VOICE** Shrill scream; twittering cries at nest colony.

DISTRIBUTION Most common in C India, east to Assam; less common south of Maharashtra, Andhra Pradesh. **HABITAT & HABITS** Occurs in large rivers; favours placid waters. Solitary or loose flocks fly over water. Characteristic hunting style is to skim over calm waters, bill wide open, the longer projecting lower mandible partly submerged at an angle, to snap up fish on striking. Many birds rest together on sandbars.

Tibetan Sandgrouse ■ *Syrrhaptes tibetanus* 48cm

DESCRIPTION Large, high-altitude, pintailed sandgrouse. Pigeon shaped with small head and bill, and feathered legs. Long, pointed wings and fast flight. Male rather pale sandy-brown, especially below. Orange face, fine black barring on breast and spots on shoulders. White belly and feet feathering. Underside of wings, flight feathers and trailing edge contrasting black. Female heavily vermiculated black from crown to rump. **FOOD** Buds, flowers and green parts of plants, especially legumes. **VOICE** Deep, musical *guk guk*. **DISTRIBUTION** Locally common breeding resident in Ladakh, Himachal Pradesh and Sikkim. Also C Asia. **HABITAT & HABITS** Inhabits high-altitude, stony pastures and semi-desert, where it is the only sandgrouse. Tame and approachable. Seldom drinks. Feeds on plant seeds. Lays eggs on bare ground. Young precocial.

Ashy Wood Pigeon ■ *Columba pulchricollis* 36cm

DESCRIPTION Creamy-buff collar, pale grey head and blackish-grey mantle diagnostic. Similar to the Speckled Wood Pigeon (opposite) but distinguished by slate-grey upperparts,

lack of white speckles on wing-coverts and uniform dark slate-grey breast. Iridescent green and purple on lower neck and back. Juvenile has more brown upperparts than adults, with less distinct patterning on neck, and rufous fringes to feathers of breast and belly. **FOOD** Mostly frugivorous and arboreal; also feeds on seeds and grains, acorns, cardamom berries and small snails. **VOICE** Call slightly booming, repeated *whuoo… whuoo…whuoo*. **DISTRIBUTION** Himalayas, hills of NE India. **HABITAT & HABITS** Found in dense foliage in broadleaved forests, occurring singly or in pairs. Sits quietly in tree canopy; disappears swiftly when flushed. Nests in flimsy structures of intertwined twigs.

Hill Pigeon ■ *Columba rupestris* 33cm

DESCRIPTION Medium-sized, pale grey pigeon with dark tail with striking, broad white subterminal band. Very similar to, but paler than, the **Rock Dove** C. *Livia*. Usually shows white lower back and shorter black wing-bars. Tail pattern diagnostic. Sexes alike. **FOOD** Mainly granivorous, feeding on weed seeds; also grains, green shoots of crops, leaves and some snails. **VOICE** Rather high-pitched *guk guk guk*. **DISTRIBUTION** Common resident in Himalayas from Kashmir to Nepal. Also C and E Asia. **HABITAT & HABITS** Inhabits high, rocky country and village cultivation. Often confiding and mixes with Rock Doves. Usually in flocks. Nests in crevice in cliff or building.

Speckled Wood Pigeon ▪ *Columba hodgsoni* 38cm

DESCRIPTION Overall very dark maroonish-brown with silvery-grey head. Grey neck heavily speckled with dark maroon-brown; maroon mantle and maroon underparts (grey in female). Distinguished from the Ashy Wood Pigeon (opposite) by lack of buff neck-patch and white spotting on wing-coverts. Juvenile similar to female, but with less distinct neck patterning. **FOOD** Mostly arboreal and frugivorous, but also takes herbs, seeds and cereals on the ground. **VOICE** Deep *whock… whr…ooooo…whroo*. **DISTRIBUTION** Himalayas, hills of NE India. **HABITAT & HABITS** Found in oak-rhododendron forests in pairs or small groups. Seen flying swiftly through forest. Feeds mainly in trees on fruits and sometimes in cultivation.

Snow Pigeon ▪ *Columba leuconota* 34cm

DESCRIPTION Medium-sized, very distinctive pale pigeon with dark grey head. White collar, underparts and rump, pale brownish back, and grey wings with three dark wing-bars. Dark grey tail with broad white chevron forming very obvious bar, particularly in flight. Sexes alike. **FOOD** Mostly herb seeds, crocus bulbs, small roots and small, hard seeds. **VOICE** High *coo coo* and various croaks. **DISTRIBUTION** Locally common breeding resident of high Himalayas. Also Tibet and China. **HABITAT & HABITS** Inhabits cliffs, gorges, steep slopes and cultivation. Forages in flocks on seeds, including cereal gleanings, and bulbs. Often feeds around snow meltwater. Strong, wheeling flight. Nests colonially on cliffs.

Yellow-footed Green Pigeon ■ *Treron phoenicopterus* 33cm

DESCRIPTION Male ashy olive-green above; olive-yellow collar, band in dark slaty tail; lilac-red shoulder-patch (mostly absent in female); yellow legs and underbody.

Female slightly duller than male. Nominate (northern) race has grey lower breast and belly. **FOOD** Fruits, including berries. **VOICE** Rich, mellow whistling notes. **DISTRIBUTION** South roughly of line from S Rajasthan to Orissa to Sri Lanka; rarer in Pakistan. **HABITAT & HABITS** Occurs in forests, orchards, city parks and cultivated village vicinities. Found in small flocks. Mostly arboreal, rarely coming to salt-licks or cropland. Remains well hidden in foliage but moves briskly. Has favourite feeding trees.

Wedge-tailed Green Pigeon ■ *Treron sphenurus* 33cm

DESCRIPTION Largish pigeon with distinctive wedge-shaped tail; dark grey-green plumage on upperparts; maroon patch of male restricted to shoulders and lower mantle; grey upper mantle; pale orange crown and breast; only faint, narrow yellow edges to wing-coverts; yellowish-green face, throat and underparts. **FOOD** Fruits, mostly figs; berries. **VOICE** Call melodious, whistling *hoo …whoo…huhuhu…* **DISTRIBUTION** Himachal Pradesh east to entire NE Indian region. **HABITAT & HABITS** Inhabits subtropical broadleaved mixed forests and edges of forests. Often associates with other green pigeons.

Emerald Dove

■ *Chalcophaps indica* 26cm

DESCRIPTION Sexes alike. Bronze emerald-green upper body; white forehead and eyebrows; grey crown and neck; white on wing shoulder and across lower back; whitish rump diagnostic in flight; rich pinkish-brown below; coral-red bill and pink-red legs. **FOOD** Seeds and fallen fruits; also termites. **VOICE** Deep, plaintive *hoo… oon…hoo…oon…*, many times at a stretch. **DISTRIBUTION** Almost throughout subcontinent to about 2,000m. Absent in Pakistan. **HABITAT & HABITS** Occurs in forest, bamboo and clearings; foothills. Solitary or in pairs. Moves on forest paths and clearings, or darts almost blindly through trees, usually under 5m off the ground. Difficult to spot on the ground.

Spotted Dove

■ *Spilopelia chinensis* 30cm

DESCRIPTION Sexes alike. Grey and pink-brown above, spotted white; white-spotted black hindneck collar (chessboard) diagnostic; dark tail with broad white tips to outer feathers seen in flight; vinous-brown breast, merging into white on belly. Young birds barred above and lack chessboard. **FOOD** Grains and seeds. **VOICE** Familiar bird sound of India: soft, somewhat doleful, *crook…cru…croo* or *croo…croo… croo*. **DISTRIBUTION** Subcontinent, to about 3,500m in Himalayas. **HABITAT & HABITS** Found in open forest, scrub, habitation and cultivation. Occurs in pairs or small parties on the ground; often settles on paths and roads, flying further on intrusion. Quite tame and confiding in many areas. Drinks often. At harvest times, seen with other doves in immense gatherings.

Laughing Dove ▪ *Spilopelia senegalensis* 26cm

DESCRIPTION Sexes alike. Pinkish grey-brown plumage with black and white chessboard

on foreneck-sides; white tips to outer-tail feathers, and broad grey wing-patches best seen in flight; small size distinctive. **FOOD** Grains, grass, weeds and seeds. **VOICE** Somewhat harsh but pleasant *cru…do…do…do…do*. **DISTRIBUTION** Almost all India to about 1,200m in outer Himalayas; uncommon in north-east states. **HABITAT & HABITS** Found in open scrub, cultivation and neighbourhood of human habitation. Occurs in pairs or small flocks. Associates freely with other doves in huge gatherings at harvest time. Feeds mostly on the ground, walking about silently.

Eurasian Collared Dove ▪ *Streptopelia decaocto* 32cm

DESCRIPTION Sexes alike. Greyish-brown plumage; lilac wash about head and neck;

black half-collar on hindneck diagnostic; broad whitish tips to brown tail feathers, seen as terminal band when fanned during landing; dull lilac breast and ashy-grey underbody. **FOOD** Seeds and grains. **VOICE** Characteristic *kukkoo…kook…*, almost dream-like in quality; also strident *koon…koon…* when male displays at breeding onset. **DISTRIBUTION** Most of area, except extreme NE Himalayas; resident and local migrant; most common in NW, W and C India. **HABITAT & HABITS** Found in cultivation, open scrub and dry forest. Occurs in small parties when not breeding. Often associates with other doves. Large gatherings glean in cultivated country. Strong flier, chasing intruders in its territory.

Red Collared Dove ▪ *Streptopelia tranquebarica* 22cm

DESCRIPTION Male: deep ashy-grey head; black hindneck collar; rich wine-red back; slaty grey-brown lower back, rump and uppertail; whitish tips to all but central tail feathers. Female: much like the Eurasian Collared Dove (opposite), but smaller size and more brownish colouration distinctive. **FOOD** Grass and other seeds; cereals. **VOICE** Quick, repeated *gru…gurgoo…* call, with more stress on first syllable. **DISTRIBUTION** Throughout area, south of Himalayan foothills. **HABITAT & HABITS** Found in cultivation, scrub and deciduous country. Solitary, or in pairs or small parties. Associates with other doves but is less common. Feeds on the ground, gleaning on harvested cropland. Perches and suns itself on leafless branches and overhead wires.

Rose-ringed Parakeet ▪ *Psittacula krameri* 42cm

DESCRIPTION Male: grass-green plumage; short, hooked red bill; rosy-pink and black collar distinctive (obtained only during third year). Female: lacks pink and black collar; instead has pale emerald-green around neck. **FOOD** Fruits, crops and cereals. **VOICE** Shrill *keeak…* screams. **DISTRIBUTION** Subcontinent, south of Himalayan foothills. **HABITAT & HABITS** Occurs in light forest, orchards, towns and villages. Gregarious; large flocks a familiar sight in India. Causes extensive damage to standing crops, orchards and garden fruit trees; also raids grain depots and markets. Large roosting colonies, often with mynas and crows.

Plum-headed Parakeet ■ *Psittacula cyanocephala* 35cm

DESCRIPTION Male: yellowish-green plumage; plum-red head; black and bluish-green collar; maroon-red wing shoulder-patch; white tips to central tail feathers distinctive. Female: dull, greyer head; yellow collar; almost non-existent maroon shoulder-patch. **FOOD** Fruits, grains, flower nectar and petals. **VOICE** Loud, interrogative *tooi…tooi…*

notes in fast flight; also other chattering notes. **DISTRIBUTION** Subcontinent south of Himalayan foothills. **HABITAT & HABITS** Found in forest, orchards and cultivation in forest. Occurs in pairs or small parties. Arboreal, but descends into cultivation in forest clearings and outskirts. Sometimes huge gatherings in cultivation. Strong, darting flight over forest.

Alexandrine Parakeet ■ *Psittacula eupatria* 52cm

DESCRIPTION Male: rich grass-green plumage; hooked, heavy red bill; deep red shoulder-patch; rose-pink collar and black stripe from lower mandible to collar distinctive. Female: smaller and lacks collar and black stripe. Yellow undertail in both sexes. **FOOD** Fruits, vegetables, crops and seeds. **VOICE** High-pitched *kreeak…* scream, on the wing as well as on perch. Popular cage bird, learning to imitate some notes and a few human words. **DISTRIBUTION** Almost throughout area, south of Himalayan foothills. **HABITAT & HABITS** Found in forest, orchards, cultivated areas and towns. Occurs in small flocks and large gatherings. Feeds on fruiting trees in orchards and on standing crops, often causing extensive damage. Strong flier. Roosts with other birds at favoured sites.

Sirkeer Malkoha

■ *Taccocua leschenaultii* 45cm

DESCRIPTION Sexes alike. Olive-brown plumage; long, graduated tail, with broad white tips to blackish outer feathers diagnostic in flight; cherry-red bill with yellow tip. **FOOD** Insects, fallen fruits and lizards. **VOICE** Fairly loud, sharp clicking notes: mostly vocal when breeding. **DISTRIBUTION** Most of subcontinent to about 1,800m in Himalayas; absent in NW India and Kashmir. **HABITAT & HABITS** Occurs in open jungle, scrub, ravines and dense growth around habitation. Runs low and rat-like when disturbed. Builds its own nest. Endemic resident of thorn scrub and semi-desert regions. Solitary or in pairs; sometimes 4–5 birds in a neighbourhood. Moves mostly on the ground, in dense growth; may clamber out on to some bush tops or low trees. Flight weak and short.

Common Hawk Cuckoo

■ *Hierococcyx varius* 35cm

DESCRIPTION Sexes alike. Ashy-grey above; dark bars on rufescent-tipped tail; dull white below, with pale ashy-rufous on breast; barred below. Young birds broadly streaked dark below; pale rufous barrings on brown upper body. **FOOD** Mainly insects; rarely wild fruits and small lizards. **VOICE** Famous call notes, interpreted as *brain-fever…*, uttered untiringly in crescendo; also described as *pipeeha…pipeeha…*; very noisy in overcast weather. **DISTRIBUTION** Subcontinent, south of Himalayan foothills; uncommon, even during rains, in arid zones. **HABITAT & HABITS** Occurs in forests, open country and near habitation. Solitary, rarely in pairs. Strictly arboreal. Noisy in May–September; silent after rains.

Jacobin Cuckoo
■ *Clamator jacobinus* 33cm

DESCRIPTION Sexes alike. Black above; noticeable crest; white in wings and white tip to long tail feathers diagnostic in flight; white underbody. Young birds, seen in autumn, dull sooty-brown with indistinct crests; white areas dull fulvous. **FOOD** Insects, including hairy, noxious caterpillars. **VOICE** Noisy; loud, metallic *plew...piu...* call notes; other shrill shrieks. **DISTRIBUTION** Chiefly south-west monsoon breeding visitor; most of area south of outer Himalayas. **HABITAT & HABITS** Occurs in open forest, cultivation and orchards. Solitary or in small parties of 4–6. Arboreal; occasionally descends to the ground to feed on insects. Arrives just before south-west monsoon by end of May. Noisy and active, with birds chasing one another. Mobbed by crows on arrival.

Asian Koel ■ *Eudynamys scolopaceus* 42cm

DESCRIPTION Male: metallic-black plumage; greenish bill and crimson eyes. Female: dark brown, thickly spotted and barred white; whitish below, dark-spotted on throat, barred below. **FOOD** *Ficus* and other fruits; insects, snails and eggs of small birds. **VOICE**

Familiar call of Indian countryside. Very noisy in March–June, coinciding with breeding of crows; loud *kuoo...kuooo...* whistling calls in crescendo by male, the first syllable longish; water-bubbling call of female. Mostly silent in July–February. **DISTRIBUTION** Subcontinent, to about 1,800m in outer Himalayas; uncommon in drier areas. **HABITAT & HABITS** Found in light forests, orchards, city parks, cultivation and open areas. Solitary or in pairs. Arboreal. Fast flight.

Indian Cuckoo

▪ *Cuculus micropterus* 32cm

DESCRIPTION Sexes alike. Slaty-brown above; greyer on head, throat and breast; whitish below, with broadly spaced black cross-bars; broad subterminal tail-band (characteristic of non-hawk cuckoos of genus *Cuculus*). Female often has rufous-brown wash on throat and breast; call notes most important identification clue. The **Eurasian Cuckoo** *C. canorus* differs from Indian by lacking subterminal black band, and has diagnostic *cuck-koo* call. **FOOD** Insects, with special fondness for hairy caterpillars. **VOICE** Very distinct call; four-note mellow whistle, variously interpreted, the best known being *bo... ko...ta...ko*, or *crossword...puzzle*; the third note trailing slightly and the fourth a little more. Very vocal in April–August, coinciding with breeding of principal hosts, drongos and orioles. May call for several minutes continuously, often throughout the day if overcast. **DISTRIBUTION** Subcontinent south from Himalayas to about 2,500m, excepting drier and arid parts of NW India; absent in Pakistan. **HABITAT & HABITS** Occurs in forest and orchards. Solitary. Arboreal and not easy to see. Overall appearance very hawk-like, but distinctly weaker looking flight.

Eurasian Cuckoo

Greater Coucal

▪ *Centropus sinensis* 50cm

DESCRIPTION Sexes alike. Glossy bluish-black plumage; chestnut wings; blackish, loose-looking, long, graduated tail. Female somewhat bigger than male. **FOOD** Insects, lizards, frogs, eggs and young of other birds, and small snakes. **VOICE** Loud and resonant *coop...coop...coop...* call familiar; occasional squeaky call. **DISTRIBUTION** Subcontinent, from outer Himalayas to about 2,000m. **HABITAT & HABITS** Found in forest, scrub, cultivation, gardens, derelict patches and vicinity of human habitation. Solitary or in pairs. Moves amid dense growth, fanning and flicking tail often. Clambers up into trees, but is a poor flier, lazily flying short distances.

Collared Scops Owl ■ *Otus (bakkamoena) lettia* 25cm

DESCRIPTION Sexes alike. Small ear-tufts and upright posture. Greyish-brown above, profusely marked whitish; buffy nuchal collar diagnostic; buffy-white underbody, streaked

and mottled dark. Very similar **Indian Scops Owl** O. *bakkamoena* mostly distinguished by its call. **FOOD** Insects, small lizards and rodents; also small birds. **VOICE** Single-note *wut…wut…*, rather questioning in tone. Calls through

ABOVE: *Indian Scops Owl*

the night, often for 20 minutes at a stretch, a *wut…*every 2–4 seconds. **DISTRIBUTION** Resident in Himalayas and NE India. **HABITAT & HABITS** Found in forests, cultivation, orchards and trees in vicinity of human habitation. Solitary or in pairs. Remains motionless by day in thick, leafy branches or at junctions of stems and branches; very difficult to spot. Flies at around dusk.

Indian Eagle Owl ■ *Bubo b. bengalensis* 56cm

DESCRIPTION Sexes alike. Brown plumage, mottled and streaked dark, and light, prominent ear-tufts; orange eyes; legs fully feathered. The **Brown Fish Owl** *Ketupa*

ABOVE: *Brown Fish Owl*

zeylonensis (56cm) darker, with white throat-patch and naked legs. **FOOD** Rodents; also reptiles, frogs and medium-sized birds. **VOICE** Deep, booming *bu… boo…* call; snapping calls at nest. **DISTRIBUTION** Throughout area, to about 1,500m in Himalayas. **HABITAT & HABITS** Found in ravines, cliffsides, riversides, scrub and open country. Solitary or in pairs. Mostly nocturnal, spending day in leafy branches, on rock ledge or in old well. Flies slowly but considerable distances when disturbed. Emerges to feed around sunset, advertising arrival with characteristic call.

Jungle Owlet ▪ *Glaucidium radiatum* 20cm

DESCRIPTION Sexes alike. Lacks ear-tufts. Darkish brown above, barred rufous and white; flight feathers barred rufous and black; white moustachial stripe, centre of breast and abdomen; remainder of underbody barred dark rufous-brown and white. The **Asian Barred Owlet** G. *cuculoides* (23cm) of Himalayas slightly larger, with abdominal streaks. **FOOD** Insects, small birds, lizards and rodents. **VOICE** Noisy; musical *kuo…kak… kuo…kak…* call notes, rising in crescendo for a few seconds only to end abruptly; other pleasant, bubbling notes. **DISTRIBUTION** Throughout area, to 2,000m in Himalayas; absent in extreme north-east states. **HABITAT & HABITS** Found in forest; partial to teak and bamboo mixed forests. Solitary or in pairs. Crepuscular, but sometimes also active and noisy by day; otherwise spends day in leafy branches. Flies short distance when disturbed.

Asian Barred Owlet

Spotted Owlet
▪ *Athene brama* 20cm

DESCRIPTION Sexes alike. No ear-tufts. Greyish-brown plumage, spotted white. Yellowish eyes; broken whitish-buff nuchal collar. Young birds more thickly marked white than adults; darkish streaks below breast. **FOOD** Insects, small rodents, lizards and birds. **VOICE** Assortment of scolding and cackling notes, screeches and chuckles. **DISTRIBUTION** Throughout area, to about 1,800m in outer Himalayas. **HABITAT & HABITS** Found in open forests, orchards, cultivation and vicinity of human habitation. Occurs in pairs or small parties. Roosts by day in leafy branches, tree cavities or cavities in walls. Active in some localities during daytime. Disturbed birds fly to neighbouring tree or branch, and bob and stare at intruder.

Savanna Nightjar ▪ *Caprimulgus affinis* 25cm

DESCRIPTION Male: grey-brown plumage, mottled dark; buffy 'V' on back, from shoulders to about centre of back; two pairs of outer-tail feathers white, with pale dusky tips; white wing-patches. Female: like male, but without white outer-tail feathers, which are barred; conspicuous rufous-buff wing-patches; call most important identification clue. **FOOD** Flying insects. **VOICE** Calls on wing as well as on perch, a fairly loud, penetrating *sweeesh* or *schweee*... **DISTRIBUTION** Throughout area, south of outer Himalayas to

about 2,000m; moves considerably locally. **HABITAT & HABITS** Found in rocky hillsides, scrub and grass country, light forests, dry streams and river beds, fallow land and cultivation. Solitary or several scattered over an open expanse. Overall behaviour like that of other nightjars. Remains motionless by day on open, rocky, grass or scrub-covered ground. Sometimes roosts on tree, along length of branch. Flies around dusk, often flying high. Drinks often.

Indian Nightjar ▪ *Caprimulgus asiaticus* 24cm

DESCRIPTION Small, rather bright nightjar with rufous collar. Similar to the **Large-tailed Nightjar** *C. macrurus* though scapular line less striking and collar obvious. Has similar white breast-patch and moustache. Both sexes have white apical tips to tail and white primary patches. Slightly shorter winged and tailed than other nightjars. Wide gape and small bill. **FOOD** Moths, dung beetles, grasshoppers, crickets and bugs. **VOICE** Loud, steady *chuck chuck chuck kerrrr* accelerating as it fades away. **DISTRIBUTION** Fairly common breeding resident throughout lowlands and Sri Lanka. Very local in Pakistan and Bangladesh. Also SE Asia, Madagascar and Aldabra Island. **HABITAT & HABITS** Inhabits dry, open scrub country with few trees but including fallow and sparse plantations. Habits as other nightjars but roosts exclusively on the ground. Often rests on tracks after dark. Lays eggs on bare ground.

Crested Treeswift ■ *Hemiprocne coronata* 23cm

DESCRIPTION Male: bluish-grey above, with faint greenish wash; chestnut sides to face and throat; ashy-grey breast, whiter below. Female: like male, but lacks chestnut on head. Backwards-curving crest and long, deeply forked tail diagnostic. **FOOD** Winged insects. **VOICE** Double-note faint scream; also parrot-like *kea… kea…* call. **DISTRIBUTION** Subcontinent, south of Himalayan foothills; absent in arid parts of NW India. **HABITAT & HABITS** Found in open deciduous forest. Occurs in pairs or small, scattered parties. Flies by day, hawking insects. Has favourite foraging areas. Flight graceful, not as fast as that of other swifts, but displaying typical swift mastery. Calls from perch and in flight. Unlike other swifts, perches on bare, higher branches. Drinks in flight from surfaces of forest pools.

Alpine Swift ■ *Tachymarptis melba* 22cm

DESCRIPTION Large, powerful, falcon-like swift with striking white belly. All dull brown, including undertail-coverts and breast-band. White throat often difficult to see (as in photo) but white belly obvious. Wings sickle shaped and short tail forked. **FOOD** Insects taken on the wing. **VOICE** Distinct, shrill trill, usually in flight when flocks are feeding. **DISTRIBUTION** Scarce breeding resident of western hills and Sri Lanka. Breeding summer records to northern hills. Widespread records from elsewhere as it wanders far for feeding. Also S Europe, Africa and W Asia. **HABITAT & HABITS** Feeds high aerially on insects, over forests, wetlands and cultivation. May come low during thunderstorms and passing weather fronts. Drinks by skimming water surfaces. Nests on tall buildings and cliffs. Often flies very high. When low, wings make audible 'swoosh'.

Red-headed Trogon
■ *Harpactes erythrocephalus* 35cm

DESCRIPTION Mainly red and fawn-brown bird with long, square-ended tail edged with black and white. Head and neck bright crimson, with white gorget and pinker underparts. Wings black, closely barred with white; rest of upperparts fawn-brown. Tail broadly edged black with narrow white outer borders to sides. **FOOD** Chiefly insects, and fruits, including berries, and leaves. **VOICE** Scaled sequence of *chaup chaup chaup* notes. **DISTRIBUTION** Scarce breeding resident in north-east, including parts of Nepal and Bangladesh. Also S China and SE Asia. **HABITAT & HABITS** Occurs in dense broadleaved forests. Difficult to see.

Indian Roller
■ *Coracias benghalensis* 31cm

DESCRIPTION Sexes alike. Pale greenish-brown above; rufous-brown breast; deep blue tail has light blue subterminal band; in flight, bright Oxford-blue wings and tail, with Cambridge-blue bands distinctive. **FOOD** Mostly insects; catches small lizards, frogs, small rodents and snakes. **VOICE** Usually silent; occasional harsh *khak…kak…kak…* notes; exuberant screeching notes and shrieks during courtship display, diving, tumbling and screaming wildly. **DISTRIBUTION** Almost entire subcontinent, south of outer Himalayas, where found to about 1,500m. **HABITAT & HABITS** Occurs in open country, cultivation, orchards and light forests. Solitary or in pairs; perches on overhead wires, bare branches, earthen mounds and small bush tops. Glides and drops on prey, or pounces suddenly. Batters prey against perch before swallowing.

Stork-billed Kingfisher
■ *Pelargopsis capensis* 38cm

DESCRIPTION Sexes alike. Enormous red bill diagnostic. Head dark grey-brown with yellowish collar on back of neck. Body pale green-blue above and brownish-yellow below. **FOOD** Fish, frogs and small birds. **VOICE** Noisy *Kee…kee…kee* repeated many times. **DISTRIBUTION** Subcontinent except drier parts of north-west. **HABITAT & HABITS** Found around canals, streams and coastal backwaters in well-wooded country. Solitary; more heard than seen. Does not normally hover.

White-throated Kingfisher ■ *Halcyon smyrnensis* 28cm

DESCRIPTION Sexes alike. Chestnut-brown head, neck and underbody below breast; bright turquoise-blue above, often with greenish tinge; black flight feathers and white wing-patch in flight; white chin, throat and breast distinctive; coral-red bill and legs. **FOOD** Insects, frogs, lizards and small rodents; occasionally fish. **VOICE** Noisy; loud, crackling laugh, often audible over crowded urban areas. Song a longish, quivering whistle, sounding as *kilililili…*, characteristic feature of hot season, when bird is breeding. **DISTRIBUTION** Subcontinent, south of outer Himalayas. **HABITAT & HABITS** Occurs in forest, cultivation, lakes and riversides; also coastal mangroves and estuaries. Solitary or scattered pairs on tops of overhead wires, poles and treetops. Often found far from water. Drops on to the ground to pick up prey. Fascinating courtship display.

Common Kingfisher ■ *Alcedo atthis* 18cm

DESCRIPTION Sexes alike. Bright blue above, greenish on wings; top of head finely banded black and blue; ferruginous cheeks, ear-coverts and white patch on neck-sides; white chin and throat, and deep ferruginous underbody distinctive; coral-red legs and

blackish bill. Various races differ in shade of blue-green on upper body. **FOOD** Fish; occasionally tadpoles and aquatic insects. **VOICE** Shrill *chichee chichee*. **DISTRIBUTION** Subcontinent, south of 2,000m in Himalayas;. **HABITAT & HABITS** Found around streams, lakes and canals; also coastal areas. Solitary or in scattered pairs. Never found away from water. Perches on pole or overhanging branch. Flies low over water, a brilliant blue streak, uttering its shrill notes. Sometimes tame and confiding. Dives for fish from perch, occasionally hovering over water before diving.

Pied Kingfisher ■ *Ceryle rudis* 30cm

DESCRIPTION Speckled black and white plumage diagnostic; black nuchal crest; double black gorget across breast in male. Female differs in having single, broken breast gorget. The **Crested Kingfishe**r *Megaceryle lugubris* of Himalayan streams and rivers identified by larger size (41cm), larger crest and white nuchal collar. **FOOD** Chiefly fish; occasionally tadpoles and water insects. **VOICE** Piercing, twittering *chirruk…chirruk…* cries in flight, sounding as if the bird is complaining. **DISTRIBUTION** Subcontinent, to about 2,000m in Himalayas. **HABITAT & HABITS** Found around streams, rivers and ponds; sometimes coastal areas. Solitary, in pairs or in small groups. Always around water, perched on poles, tree stumps or rocks. Hovers when hunting, bill pointed down as wings beat rapidly. Dives fast, headlong on sighting fish; batters catch on perch. Calls in flight.

ABOVE: *Crested Kingfisher*

Green Bee-eater
■ *Merops orientalis* 21cm

DESCRIPTION Sexes alike. Bright green plumage;
red-brown wash about head; pale blue on chin and
throat, bordered below by black gorget; slender,
curved black bill; rufous wash on black-tipped flight
feathers; elongated central tail feathers distinctive.
FOOD Mostly winged insects; nuisance to honey
industry. **VOICE** Noisy; cheerful trilling notes,
mainly uttered on the wing. **DISTRIBUTION**
Subcontinent, south of about 1,800m in outer
Himalayas. **HABITAT & HABITS** Found in open
country and cultivation; also light forests, city parks
and gardens. Occurs in small parties. Perches freely
on bare branches and overhead telegraph wires.
Attends to grazing cattle, with drongos, cattle egrets
and mynas. Launches graceful sorties after winged
insects; batters prey against perch before swallowing.

Blue-bearded Bee-eater
■ *Nyctyornis athertoni* 34cm

DESCRIPTION Large green bee-eater
with blue throat and long, square-ended
tail. Overall rather pale green with bluish
wash to face, shaggy throat and upper
breast. Green-streaked buff underparts.
Pale orange undertail. Powerful, decurved
dark bill. Often sits in shade, when can
look very dark. **FOOD** Winged insects; seen
on *Erythrina* and *Salmalia* flowers. **VOICE**
Deep *korrr korrr* and various chuckling
notes. **DISTRIBUTION** Scarce breeding
resident of Western and Eastern Ghats,
Himalayan foothills and north-east. Also S
China and SE Asia. **HABITAT & HABITS**
Inhabits wet forest edges. Sluggish and
shy, keeping to treetops; often along forest
roads and in clearings, and frequently in
small groups. Catches aerial insects from
perch and batters them before swallowing.
Excavates deep tunnel for nest in bank,
often in road cuttings.

Chestnut-headed Bee-eater
■ *Merops leschenaulti* 21cm

DESCRIPTION Sexes alike. Grass-green plumage; chestnut-cinnamon crown, hindneck and upper back; yellow chin and throat; rufous and black gorget. **FOOD** Chiefly winged insects, captured in flight. **VOICE** Musical twittering notes, mostly on the wing, and sometimes from perch. **DISTRIBUTION** Disjunct. Himalayan foothills country, from Uttarakhand to extreme north-east; second population in Western Ghats south of Goa; also Sri Lanka. May be seen in peninsula, especially during monsoon. **HABITAT & HABITS** Occurs in vicinity of water in forested areas. Small gatherings on telegraph wires or bare upper branches of trees, from where birds launch short aerial sallies. Fast, graceful flight. Noisy when converging at roosting trees.

Common Hoopoe ■ *Upupa epops* 31cm

DESCRIPTION Sexes alike. Fawn-coloured plumage; black and white markings on wings, back and tail; black and white-tipped crest; longish, gently curved bill. Several races. **FOOD** Insects caught on the ground or pulled from underground. **VOICE** Pleasant, mellow

hoo…po…po…, sometimes only first two notes; calls have slightly ventriloquistic quality. Calls frequently when breeding. **DISTRIBUTION** Subcontinent, to about 5,500m in Himalayas; spreads considerably in winter. **HABITAT & HABITS** Occurs in meadows, open country, garden lawns and open light forests. Solitary or in scattered pairs; small, loose flocks in winter. Probes the ground with long bill, sometimes feeding with other birds. Flits among tree branches. Crest often fanned open. Becomes rather aggressive with onset of breeding season.

Indian Grey Hornbill

■ *Ocyceros birostris* 60cm

DESCRIPTION Grey-brown plumage; large, curved bill with casque diagnostic; long, graduated tail, tipped black and white. Casque smaller in female than male. **FOOD** Fruits, lizards, insects and rodents. **VOICE** Noisy; normal call a shrill squealing note; also other squeals and screams. **DISTRIBUTION** Almost throughout India, to about 1,500m in Himalayas; absent in arid north-west regions and heavy rainfall areas of southern Western Ghats. **HABITAT & HABITS** Found in forests, orchards, tree-covered avenues and vicinity of human habitation. Occurs in pairs or small parties; sometimes large gatherings. Mostly arboreal, but descends to pick fallen fruits or lizards. Feeds with frugivorous birds on fruiting trees. Noisy, undulating flight.

Great Hornbill ■ *Buceros bicornis* 130cm

DESCRIPTION Sexes alike. Black face, back and underbody; two white bars on black wings; white neck, lower abdomen and tail; broad black tail-band; huge black and yellow bill with distinctive, enormous concave-topped casque. Female slightly smaller than male. **FOOD** Fruits, lizards, rodents and snakes. **VOICE** Loud, deep barking calls; loud *tokk* at feeding sites, audible for some distance. **DISTRIBUTION** Lower Himalayas east of Uttarakhand, to about 1,800m; another population in Western Ghats, south of Khandala. **HABITAT & HABITS** Found in forests, in pairs or small parties; occasionally large flocks. Mostly arboreal, feeding on fruiting trees, plucking fruit with tip of bill, tossing it up, catching it in throat and swallowing it. May settle on the ground to pick up fallen fruits. Noisy flight, audible from over a kilometre away, even when flying very high, caused by drone of air rushing through bases of outer quills of wing feathers. Flight an alternation of flapping and gliding, less undulating than in other hornbills.

Oriental Pied Hornbill ■ *Anthracoceros albirostris* 88cm

DESCRIPTION Sexes alike. Female slightly smaller than male. Black above; white face-patch, wing-tips (seen in flight) and tips to outer-tail feathers; black throat and breast; white below. Black and yellow bill with large casque. The **Malabar Pied Hornbill** *A. coronatus* (92cm) very similar, except for completely white outer-tail feathers. **FOOD** Fruits, lizards, snakes, young birds and insects. **VOICE** Loud cackles and screams; also rapid *pak… pak…pak*. **DISTRIBUTION** Haryana and Uttarakhand to extreme north-east; Eastern Ghats, south to Bastar and Andhra Pradesh. Malabar Pied is absent in north-east regions, but is found over Western Ghats. **HABITAT & HABITS** Inhabits forests, orchards and groves. Occurs in small parties, occasionally collecting into several dozen birds on favourite fruiting trees. Associates with other birds. Arboreal but often feeds on the ground, hopping about.

ABOVE: *Malabar Pied Hornbill*

Great Barbet ■ *Psilopogon virens* 33cm

DESCRIPTION Sexes alike. Bluish-black head and throat; maroon-brown back; yellowish hind-collar; green on lower back and tail; brown upper breast; pale yellow below, with thick, greenish-blue streaks; red undertail-coverts distinctive. Large yellowish bill. **FOOD** Fruits and flower petals. **VOICE** Very noisy, especially in March–July; loud, if somewhat mournful *pi…you* or *pi…oo*, uttered continuously for several minutes; one of the most familiar bird calls in Himalayas. Often joined by similar but high-pitched, more nasal calls of the **Golden-throated Barbet** *P. franklinii* (23cm), of E Himalayas. **DISTRIBUTION** Himalayas, 800–3,200m. **HABITAT & HABITS** Found in forests and orchards. Solitary or in small bands. Arboreal, but comes into low-fruiting bushes. Difficult to spot and mostly heard.

RIGHT: *Golden-throated Barbet*

Brown-headed Barbet ■ *Psilopogon zeylanicus* 28cm

DESCRIPTION Sexes alike. Grass-green plumage; brownish head, neck and upper back, streaked white; bare orange patch around eye. The **White-cheeked Barbet** M. *viridis* (23cm) of S India has white cheek-stripe. **FOOD** Mainly fruits; also flower nectar, petals, insects and small lizards. **VOICE** Noisy; *kutroo…kutroo* or *pukrook…pukrook* calls one of most familiar sounds of Indian forests; calls often begin with guttural *kurrrr*. **DISTRIBUTION** Most of India south of Himalayan foothills (Himachal Pradesh to Nepal). **HABITAT & HABITS** Inhabits forests and groves; also city

gardens. Solitary or in pairs; occasionally small parties. Strictly arboreal; keeps to fruiting trees, often with other frugivorous birds. Difficult to spot in canopy. Noisy in hot season; strong, undulating flight.

White-cheeked Barbet

Blue-throated Barbet

■ *Psilopogon asiaticus* 23cm

DESCRIPTION Sexes alike. Grass-green plumage; black, crimson, yellow and blue about head; blue chin and throat diagnostic; crimson spots on throat-sides. **FOOD** Mainly fruits; also insects. **VOICE** Calls similar to Brown-headed Barbet's (above) of plains. On careful hearing, sounds somewhat softer and there is a short note between the two longer ones; can be interpreted as *kutt…oo…ruk…*; also four-note song when breeding. **DISTRIBUTION** Himalayas east from Pakistan and Kashmir, to about 2,250m; also Bengal, including Kolkata. **HABITAT & HABITS** Occurs in forests and groves. Solitary or in pairs; sometimes small parties on fruiting trees, along with other fruit-eating birds. Strictly arboreal; keeps to canopy of tall trees. Difficult to spot but loud, monotonous calls an indicator of its presence.

Coppersmith Barbet ◼ *Psilopogon haemacephalus* 17cm

DESCRIPTION Sexes alike. Grass-green plumage; yellow throat; crimson breast and

forehead; dumpy appearance. **FOOD** Mainly fruits, including berries; sometimes catches insects. **VOICE** Noisy in December–end of April. Monotonous *tuk…tuk…* calls one of best-known bird calls of India, likened to coppersmith working on metal. **DISTRIBUTION** All India, to about 1,800m in outer Himalayas. **HABITAT & HABITS** Occurs in light forests, groves, city gardens and roadside trees. Solitary, in pairs or in small parties. Strictly arboreal; feeds on fruiting trees, often with other birds. Visits flowering *Erythrina* and *Bombax* trees for flower nectar; often spends early morning sunning itself on bare branches.

Speckled Piculet ◼ *Picumnus innominatus* 10cm

DESCRIPTION Sexes alike. Olive-green above (male has some orange and black on forecrown); two white stripes on head-sides, the upper one longer; dark-olive band through eyes; moustachial stripe; creamy-white below, boldly spotted with black. **FOOD** Mainly ants and termites. **VOICE** Sharp, rapid *tsip…tsip…*; also loud drumming sound. **DISTRIBUTION** Himalayas, west to east, foothills to at least 2,500m. Slightly duller southern race

malayorum has wide distribution over Eastern and Western Ghats, south of Goa; also Nilgiris, Palnis and associated mountain ranges. **HABITAT & HABITS** Occurs in mixed forests, favouring bamboo jungle. Usually in pairs; moves around thin branches, or clings upside down. Taps with bill and probes crevices. Typical woodpecker behaviour. Associates in mixed hunting bands. Unobtrusive, hence often overlooked. Perches across branches.

Brown-capped Pygmy Woodpecker ■ *Yungipicus nanus* 13cm

ABOVE: *Grey-capped Pygmy Woodpecker*

DESCRIPTION Small woodpecker. Male: barred brown and white above; paler crown with short scarlet streak (occipital); prominent white band from just above eyes extends to neck; pale dirty-brown-white below, streaked black. Female: like male but lacks scarlet streaks on crown-sides. The male **Grey-capped Pygmy Woodpecker** *Y. canicapillus* (14cm) of Himalayas has short scarlet occipital crest; black upper back and white-barred lower back and rump. **FOOD** Small insects and grubs, obtained from crevices and under bark; also small berries. **VOICE** Faint but shrill squeak; sounds like *clicck…rrr*. **DISTRIBUTION** Almost all over India, including some drier regions. **HABITAT & HABITS** Found in light forests, cultivation, bamboos and orchards; also vicinity of human habitation. Mostly in pairs. Often part of mixed bird parties in forest. Seen most often on small trees, branches and twigs, close to the ground and also high in canopy; quite active.

Streak-throated Woodpecker

■ *Picus xanthopygaeus* 30cm

DESCRIPTION Male: grass-green above; crimson crown and crest; orange and black on nape; white supercilium and malar stripe; yellow rump; bold black scaly streaks on whitish underbody, with tawny-green wash on breast; throat greyer, also streaked. Female: black crown and crest. **FOOD** Mostly insects: ants, termites and wood-boring beetle larvae; also figs. **VOICE** Occasional faint *pick…* but mostly silent; also drums on branches. **DISTRIBUTION** All subcontinent; to 1,500m in outer Himalayas. **HABITAT & HABITS** Found in mixed forests and plantations. Solitary or in pairs. Works up along tree stems; moves straight up or in spirals. Taps with bill for insects hiding in bark. Also settles on the ground.

Himalayan Woodpecker
■ *Dendrocopos himalayensis* 25cm

DESCRIPTION Male: black back and upper body; white shoulder-patch; white spots and barring on wings; crimson crown and crest; white lores, cheeks and ear-coverts; broad black moustachial stripe; yellowish-brown underbody, darker on breast; crimson undertail. Female: black crown and crest. **FOOD** Mostly insects hunted from under bark and moss; seeds of conifers; nuts and acorns. **VOICE** Fairly loud calls, uttered in night. **DISTRIBUTION** Himalayas, from Kashmir to W Nepal; 1,500–3,200m. **HABITAT & HABITS** Occurs in Himalayan forests. Mostly in pairs, moving about in forest. Jerkily moves up and around tree stems or clings to undersides of branches. Like other woodpeckers, often moves a few steps back, as if to re-examine. Sometimes seen in mixed hunting parties of Himalayan birds.

Rufous Woodpecker ■ *Micropternus brachyurus* 25cm

DESCRIPTION Sexes alike. Chestnut-brown plumage; fine black cross-bars on upper body, including wings and tail; paler edges to throat feathers; crimson patch under eye in

male, absent in female. **FOOD** Chiefly tree ants and their pupae; occasionally figs and other fruits. Seen to suck sap from near bases of banana leaves. **VOICE** Rather vocal in January–April. Loud, high-pitched 3–4 notes, *ke…ke…kr…ke…*; drums when breeding. **DISTRIBUTION** Subcontinent, south of outer Himalayas, to 1,500m. **HABITAT**

& HABITS Mixed forests. Usually in pairs; sometimes 4–5 scattered birds close by. Mostly seen around ball-shaped nests of tree ants; clings to outsides of nests and digs for ants. Plumage often smeared with gummy substance.

Yellow-crowned Woodpecker

■ *Leiopicus mahrattensis* 18cm

DESCRIPTION Male: brownish-black above, spotted all over with white; golden-brown forehead and crown; small scarlet crest; pale fulvous below throat, streaked brown; scarlet patch in centre of abdomen distinctive. Female: lacks scarlet crest. **FOOD** Chiefly insects; also figs, other fruits and flower nectar. **VOICE** Soft but sharp *clic…click…clickrrr…*; drums when breeding. **DISTRIBUTION** Common and widespread; almost subcontinent, from Himalayan foothills south; uncommon in north-east regions. **HABITAT & HABITS** Occurs in open forests, scrub, cultivation, vicinity of human habitation and gardens. Solitary or in pairs; sometimes small bands of up to six birds. Occasionally with mixed hunting parties. Moves in jerks along tree stems and branches. Hunts in typical woodpecker manner. Rather confiding in some areas. Birds keep in touch with faint creaking sounds.

Greater Yellownape

■ *Chrysophlegma flavinucha* 16cm

DESCRIPTION Similar to the **Lesser Yellownape** *Picus chlorolophus* but larger. Lesser has smaller, dark bill, red markings on head, red stripe on whitish chin, smaller crest and barred underparts; prominent yellow-crested nape and throat. Underparts dark olive-green and grey. Brownish crown; flight feathers chestnut-barred black. **FOOD** Ants and termites, and large insect larvae, particularly of wood-boring beetles. **VOICE** Calls include loud, plaintive *keeyu* and hard *chep* note. Also, accelerating trill, *quee… quee… quee*. **DISTRIBUTION** Fairly common breeding resident of foothills, NE India, Bangladesh and Eastern Ghats. **HABITAT & HABITS** Upland broadleaved forests. Feeds on invertebrates from the ground to canopy, often with mixed species parties. Shy, flushing readily if disturbed. Uses tail as prop. Nests in tree holes.

Grey-headed Woodpecker
■ *Picus canus* 32cm

DESCRIPTION Male: darkish green above; crimson forehead; black hindcrown, faint crest and nape; dark sides of head and black malar stripe; yellow rump; white-barred dark wings and blackish tail; unmarked; dull greyish-olive underbody diagnostic. Female: black from forehead to nape; no crimson. FOOD Termites, ants, and wood-boring beetles and their larvae; also flower nectar and fruits. VOICE Loud, chattering alarm; common call high-pitched *keek…keek…* of 4 or 5 notes. Drums often in March–early June. DISTRIBUTION Himalayas from lower foothills country to about 2,700m. HABITAT & HABITS Inhabits deciduous and temperate forests. Solitary or in pairs. Typical woodpecker, moving on tree stems and larger branches, hunting out insects from under bark. Descends to the ground, hopping awkwardly. Also digs into termite mounds.

Black-rumped Flameback
■ *Dinopium benghalense* 30cm

DESCRIPTION Male: shining golden-yellow and black above; crimson crown and crest; black throat and head-sides, with fine white streaks; white underbody, streaked black, boldly on breast. Female: black crown spotted with white; crimson crest. FOOD Mainly ants and termites; caterpillars and centipedes on the ground; also figs and berries. VOICE Noisy; loud, high-pitched cackle, like laughter. Drums often. DISTRIBUTION Subcontinent, to about 1,800m in outer Himalayas; also drier areas of NW India. HABITAT & HABITS Found in dry and mixed deciduous forests, orchards, gardens, and neighbourhoods of villages and other human habitation. Usually in pairs; sometimes half a dozen together. Widespread and common; moves jerkily up and around tree stems or clings to undersides of branches. Taps out insects. Often associates in mixed hunting parties. May descend to the ground, picking off ants and other insects.

Greater Flameback ▪ *Chrysocolaptes guttacristatus* 32cm

DESCRIPTION Male: crimson crown and crest; golden-olive above; white and black sides of face and throat; whitish-buff below, profusely spotted with black on foreneck, and speckled over rest of underbody; extensive crimson rump, and black tail and flight feathers distinctive. Female: white-spotted black crown and crest. The **Himalayan Flameback** *Dinopium shorii* very similar, but slightly smaller, and black nape, three toes and two narrow stripes down throat-centre can help make the distinction. **FOOD** Insects; possibly nectar. **VOICE** Noisy; loud, grating scream; calls mostly in flight. **DISTRIBUTION** Uttarakhand to north-east; parts of Eastern Ghats, SE Madhya Pradesh; Western Ghats, Kerala to Tapti river; plains to about 1,500m. **HABITAT & HABITS** Inhabits forests. Occurs in pairs or small bands. Arboreal; moves jerkily up along tree stems.

Himalayan Goldenback

Indian Pitta ▪ *Pitta brachyura* 19cm

DESCRIPTION Sexes alike. Multi-coloured, stub-tailed, stoutly built bird; bright blue, green, black, white, yellowish-brown and crimson; white chin, throat and patch on wing-tips, and crimson vent, distinctive. **FOOD** Mainly insects. **VOICE** Loud, lively whistle, *wheeet…peu*. Very vocal when breeding (during rains). Also longish single-note whistle. **DISTRIBUTION** Almost entire subcontinent, with considerable seasonal movement, particularly before and after rains; breeds commonly in C India; also elsewhere. **HABITAT & HABITS** Inhabits forests and orchards; also cultivated country. Solitary or in pairs; small flocks on migration, before and after monsoons. Spends much time on the ground, hopping about, hunting for insects among leaf litter and low herbage. Quietly flies into tree branch if disturbed. Favours shaded, semi-damp areas.

Common Woodshrike ▪ *Tephrodornis pondicerianus* 16cm

DESCRIPTION Sexes alike. Greyish-brown plumage; broad whitish supercilium and dark stripe below eye distinctive; white outer-tail feathers seen in flight. Dark stripe may

be slightly paler in female than male. The **Malabar Wood Shrike** *T. p. sylvicola* (23cm) has white outer-tail feathers. **FOOD** Insects; also flower nectar. **VOICE** Whistling *wheet… wheet…* and interrogative, quick-repeated *whi…whi… whi…whee* thereafter. Other trilling, pleasant notes when breeding. **DISTRIBUTION** Most of the country, south of

Himalayan foothills; most common in low country. **HABITAT & HABITS** Found in light forests, forest edges, cultivation, and gardens in and around human habitation. Occurs in pairs or small parties. Quiet for greater part of year, and vocal when breeding (February–May). Keeps to middle levels of trees, hopping about, sometimes coming to the ground.

LEFT: *Malabar Wood Shrike*

Common Iora ▪ *Aegithina tiphia* 14cm

DESCRIPTION Male: greenish above (rich black above, with yellowish rump, in summer breeding plumage); black wings and tail; two white wing-bars; bright yellow underbody. Female: yellow-green plumage; white wing-bars; greenish-brown wings. **FOOD** Insects and spiders; also flower nectar. **VOICE** Renowned vocalist; wide range of rich, whistling notes; single or two-note, long-drawn *wheeeeeee* or *wheeeeeee…chu* a common call; another is a three-note whistle. **DISTRIBUTION** Subcontinent, to about 1,800m in Himalayas; absent in arid north-west, desert regions of Rajasthan, Kutch. **HABITAT & HABITS** Occurs in forest, gardens, orchards and tree-dotted cultivation. Pairs keep to leafy branches, often with other small birds. Moves energetically among branches in hunt for insects and caterpillars. Rich call notes often a giveaway of its presence in an area.

Short-billed Minivet
■ *Pericrocotus brevirostris* 19cm

DESCRIPTION Adult male has black hood, throat, mantle and wings; deep red underparts; similar to the **Long-tailed Minivet** *P. ethologus*, shorter tail, like the Scarlet Minivet's (below) but smaller, more slender; wings lack red spots or 'drops' on tips of tertials, secondaries. Female brighter yellow below than male, including on throat; no wing-spots; more yellow on forehead, including forecrown; yellower cheeks. **FOOD** Insects and buds. **VOICE** Call a high-whistled *tsee…tup*. **DISTRIBUTION** C Nepal eastwards. S Assam Hills. **HABITAT** Open broadleaved forests; edges of forests; secondary growth.

Scarlet Minivet ■ *Pericrocotus (flammeus) speciosus* 20cm

DESCRIPTION Male: glistening black head and upper back; deep scarlet lower back and rump; black and scarlet wings and tail; black throat, scarlet below. Female: rich yellow forehead, supercilium; grey-yellow above; yellow and black wings and tail; bright yellow underbody. **FOOD** Insects and flower nectar. **VOICE** Pleasant, two-note whistle; also longer, whistling warble. **DISTRIBUTION** Disjunct; several isolated races. The recently split **Orange Minivet** *P. flammeus* is found south of Gujarat through Western Ghats. **HABITAT & HABITS** Found in forests, gardens and groves. Occurs in pairs or small parties; sometimes several dozen together. Keeps to canopy of tall trees. Actively flits about to hunt for insects; also launches aerial sallies after winged insects. Often seen in mixed hunting parties of birds; spectacular sight of black, scarlet and yellow as flock flies over forest, especially when seen from above.

Brown Shrike

■ *Lanius cristatus* 19cm

DESCRIPTION Uniformly rufous-brown upperparts; black band through eye with white brow over it. Pale creamy underside with warmer rufous flanks; rufous tail. Wings brown without any white 'mirror'. Female has faint scalloping on underside. **FOOD** Insects, lizards and small rodents. **VOICE** Harsh chattering; grating call; sometimes sings in low, chirruping tone with bill closed. **DISTRIBUTION** Winter visitor to peninsular India. **HABITAT & HABITS** Open country, cultivation, forest edges, scrub and gardens. Solitary. Keeps lookout from conspicuous perch or tree stump for prey on the ground, often returning to same perch after hunting. Territorial.

Bay-backed Shrike

■ *Lanius vittatus* 18cm

DESCRIPTION Sexes alike. Deep chestnut-maroon back; broad black forehead-band, continuing through eyes to ear-coverts; grey crown and neck, separated from black by small white patch; white rump distinctive; black wings with white in outer flight feathers; white underbody, fulvous on breast and flanks. **FOOD** Insects, lizards and small rodents. **VOICE** Harsh *churr*; breeding male has lively warble. Sometimes imitates other bird calls. **DISTRIBUTION** Subcontinent, to about 1,800m in Himalayas; absent in north-east. **HABITAT & HABITS** Occurs in open country, light forests and scrub. Solitary or in scattered pairs in open terrain. Keeps lookout from perch on tree stump, overhead wire or bush top, usually under 4m off the ground; pounces once potential prey is sighted. Usually devours prey on the ground, tearing it; sometimes carries it to perch. Keeps to fixed territories, defended aggressively.

Long-tailed Shrike ■ *Lanius schach* 25crn

DESCRIPTION Sexes alike. Pale grey from crown to middle of back; bright rufous from then on to rump; black forehead, band through eye; white 'mirror' in black wings; whitish underbody, tinged pale rufous on lower breast and flanks. **FOOD** Insects, lizards, small rodents and birds. **VOICE** Noisy; harsh mix of scolding notes, shrieks and yelps; excellent mimic; breeding male has rather musical song. **DISTRIBUTION** Three races; undergo considerable seasonal movement; subcontinent, from about 2,700m in Himalayas. Black-headed subspecies *L. s. tricolor* has black head and small white patch on wings; breeds in Himalayas east of Uttarakhand. **HABITAT & HABITS** Inhabits open country, cultivation, edges of forest, vicinity of human habitation and gardens; prefers neighbourhood of water. Mostly solitary. Boldly defends feeding territory. Keeps lookout from conspicuous perch; pounces on to the ground on sighting prey. Said to store surplus in 'larder', impaling prey on thorns, hence the nickname butcher-bird.

L. s. tricolor

Maroon Oriole ■ *Oriolus traillii* 27cm

DESCRIPTION Large dark oriole with chestnut-red tail. Powerful, decurved grey bill and whitish irises. Male has maroon body, and black head and wings. Female blackish above with dull maroon back and heavily brownish-streaked, white underparts. **FOOD** Insects, fruits and nectar. **VOICE** Most commonly cat-like squawking *meow*. Also fluty *pi lio ilo*. **DISTRIBUTION** Locally common breeding resident in northern hills from Himachal Pradesh east to Myanmar border. Moves lower down to foothills and nearby plains, including Bangladesh, in winter. Also S and E China, and SE Asia. **HABITAT & HABITS** Inhabits thick broadleaved forest, usually keeping well hidden in canopy. Comes into open to feed on Silk Cotton and other nectar (as shown), when it can be confiding. Usually occurs in pairs or singly; often in mixed hunting groups. Nests high in tree.

Indian Golden Oriole ■ *Oriolus (oriolus) kundoo* 25cm

DESCRIPTION Male: bright golden-yellow plumage; black stripe through eye; black wings and centre of tail. Female: yellow-green above; brownish-green wings; dirty-white below, streaked brown. Young male much like female. **FOOD** Insects, fruits and nectar. **VOICE** Fluty whistle of 2–3 notes, *pee…lo…lo,* the middle note lower; harsh note often

heard. Rich, mellow song when breeding, somewhat mournful; does not sing often. **DISTRIBUTION** Summer visitor to Himalayan foothills to about 2,600m, spreading in winter to plains; also breeds in many parts of peninsula. **HABITAT & HABITS** Inhabits forest, orchards and gardens around habitation. Solitary or in pairs. Arboreal, sometimes moving with other birds in upper branches. Regularly visits fruiting and flowering trees. Hunts insects in leafy branches. Usually heard, and surprisingly not often seen, despite bright colour; seen only when it emerges on bare branch or flies across.

Black-hooded Oriole

■ *Orialus xanthornus* 25cm

DESCRIPTION Sexes alike. Golden-yellow plumage; black head diagnostic; black and yellow wings and tail; deep pink-red bill seen at close quarters. **FOOD** Fruits, flower nectar and insects. **VOICE** Assortment of melodious and harsh calls; most common is fluty 2–3-noted *tu…hee* or *tll…yow…yow…;* also single, mellow note. **DISTRIBUTION** Subcontinent, to about 1,000m in Himalayan foothills. **HABITAT & HABITS** Found in forests, orchards and gardens, often amid habitation. Occurs in pairs or small parties. Strictly arboreal, rarely descending into lower bushes or to the ground. Active and lively. Moves a lot in forest and birds chase one another, the rich colours striking against green or brown of forest. Very vocal. Associates with other birds in mixed parties. Visits fruiting and flowering trees.

Black Drongo ▪ *Dicrurus macrocercus* 28cm

DESCRIPTION Sexes alike. Glossy black plumage; long, deeply forked tail. Diagnostic white spot at bill-base. The **Ashy Drongo** *D. leucophaeus* (30cm) grey-black, and more of a forest bird, breeding in Himalayas and a winter visitor to peninsula. **FOOD** Mainly insects, supplemented with flower nectar and small lizards. **VOICE** Harsh *tiu-tiu;* also *cheece cheece*. **DISTRIBUTION** Subcontinent, to about 1,800m in outer Himalayas. **HABITAT & HABITS** Found in open country, orchards and cultivation. Usually solitary; sometimes in small parties. Keeps lookout from exposed perch. Most common bird seen on rail and road travel in India. Drops to the ground to capture prey. Launches short aerial sallies. Rides on grazing cattle. Follows cattle, tractors, grass-cutters and fires; thus consumes vast numbers of insects. Bold and aggressive species, with several birds nesting in same tree.

Ashy Drongo

Spangled Drongo
▪ *Dicrurus hottentottus* 30cm

DESCRIPTION Sexes alike. Glistening blue-black plumage, fine, hair-like feathers on forehead; longish, downcurved, pointed bill; diagnostic tail, square-cut and inwardly bent (curling) towards outer ends. **FOOD** Mainly flower nectar; also insects, more so when there are young in nest. **VOICE** Noisy; mix of whistling, metallic calls and harsh screams. **DISTRIBUTION** Lower Himalayan foothills, east of Uttarakhand; down through NE India, along Eastern Ghats, Orissa, Bastar through to Western Ghats, up north to Mumbai, occasionally even further north. **HABITAT & HABITS** Inhabits forests. Solitary or in scattered pairs. Strictly arboreal forest bird. Small numbers may gather on favourite flowering trees. Rather aggressive. Often seen in mixed hunting parties of birds.

Greater Racquet-tailed Drongo ■ *Dicrurus paradiseus* 60cm

DESCRIPTION Sexes alike. Glossy blue-black plumage; prominent crest of longish feathers, curving backwards; elongated, wire-like outer-tail feathers, ending in 'rackets', diagnostic. The **Lesser Racquet-tailed Drongo** *D. remifer* (38cm) found in lower Himalayas, east of Uttarakhand. **FOOD** Mostly insects; also lizards and flower nectar. **VOICE** Noisiest bird of forest. Amazing mimic, with wide variety of whistles and screams, and perfect imitations of over a dozen species. **DISTRIBUTION** Found in forested parts of India, roughly east and south of line from S Gujarat to Uttarakhand, to about 1,400m. **HABITAT & HABITS** Found in forests; also forest edges and orchards. Solitary or in pairs; sometimes small gatherings. Arboreal forest bird, but often descends into low bush. Moves a lot in forest. Confirmed exhibitionist, both by sight and sound. Very noisy; often vocal long before sunrise. Bold and aggressive; seen mobbing bigger birds 100m over forest.

ABOVE RIGHT: *Lesser Racquet-tailed Drongo*

White-throated Fantail ■ *Rhipidura albicollis* 17cm

DESCRIPTION Sexes alike. Slaty-brown plumage, including underbody; short white supercilium; white throat and tips to all but central tail feathers. The **White-spotted Fantail** *R. albogularis* has white-spotted slaty band across breast; also whitish-buff belly, and less white on tail-tip. **FOOD** Insects and spiders. **VOICE** Harsh *chukrrr...* note. **DISTRIBUTION** Outer Himalayas, to about 1,800m; north-east regions; absent through Indo-Gangetic Plain west to north-west parts of India; two races from Orissa to Godavari river; most widespread is White-spotted race *albogularis*, found all over peninsular India, south of line from S Rajasthan, across Vindhya and south along edge of Eastern Ghats. **HABITAT & HABITS** Found in light forests, groves, gardens among habitation and scrub. Overall behaviour not appreciably different from that of **White-browed Fantail** *R. aureola*.

ABOVE: *White-spotted Fantail*   *White-browed Fantail*

Black-naped Monarch
■ *Hypothymis azurea* 16cm

DESCRIPTION Male: lilac-blue plumage; black patch on nape; gorget on breast; slight black scaly markings on crown; sooty on wings and tail; white below breast. Female: ashy-blue, duller than male; lacks black on nape and breast. **FOOD** Insects. **VOICE** Common call a sharp, grating, high-pitched *chwich…chweech* or *chwae… chweech*, slightly interrogative in tone, the two notes quickly uttered. Short, rambling notes when breeding. **DISTRIBUTION** India south of outer Himalayas, to about 1,200m, east of W Uttarakhand; absent in arid north-west, and India. **HABITAT & HABITS** Found in forest, bamboo and gardens. Solitary or in pairs in forest, often in mixed hunting parties. Very active and fidgety. Flits and flutters about, often fanning tail slightly. Calls often as it moves about, with calls often the first indication of its presence.

Indian Paradise-flycatcher ■ *Terpsiphone paradisi*
Adult male: 50cm including tail streamers

DESCRIPTION Glossy blue-black head, crest and throat; black in wings; silvery-white body, long tail streamers. In rufous phase white parts replaced by rufous-chestnut. Female and young male: 20cm. No tail streamers; shorter crest; rufous above; ashy-grey throat and nuchal collar; whitish below. **FOOD** Insects and spiders. **VOICE**

Sharp, grating *chwae* or *chchwae…* call. Melodious warbling song and display in breeding male. **DISTRIBUTION** Himalayas, foothills to about 1,800m, rarely 2,500m; India, south to Bharatpur; absent in broad belt across Gangetic Plain; widespread in peninsular India. **HABITAT & HABITS** Found in light forests, gardens and open country. Solitary or in pairs. Makes short sallies. Flits through trees, with tail streamers floating. Strictly arboreal, sometimes descending into taller bushes. Cheerful disposition.

Eurasian Jay ■ *Garrulus glandarius* 33cm

DESCRIPTION Sexes alike. Pinkish-brown plumage; velvet-black malar stripe; closely black-barred blue wings; white rump contrasts with jet-black tail. The **Black-headed Jay** G. *lanceolatus* of W Himalayas, east to about C Nepal, has black cap, black and white face, and white in wings. **FOOD** Insects, fruits and nuts. **VOICE** Noisy; guttural chuckles, screeching notes and whistles; good mimic. **DISTRIBUTION** Across Himalayas, 1,500–2,800m, somewhat higher in east; may descend low in winter. **HABITAT & HABITS** Inhabits mixed temperate forests. Occurs in small, noisy bands, often with other Himalayan birds. Common and familiar around Himalayan hill stations. Inquisitive and aggressive. Mostly keeps to trees, but also descends into bushes and on to the ground. Laboured flight.

LEFT: *Black-headed Jay*

Yellow-billed Blue Magpie
■ *Urocissa flavirostris* 66cm

DESCRIPTION Sexes alike. Purple-blue plumage; black head and breast; white nape-patch and underbody; very long, white-tipped tail; yellow bill and orange legs. The **Red-billed Blue Magpie** U. *erythrorhyncha* (70cm) has more white on nape; red bill and legs; appears to be restricted to Himalayas between Himachal Pradesh and E Nepal and some parts of NE India. **FOOD** Insects, fruits, lizards, eggs and small birds. **VOICE** Noisy; great mix of metallic screams, loud whistles and raucous notes, often imitating other birds. **DISTRIBUTION** Himalayas, west to east; 1,500–3,600m; may descend low in winter. **HABITAT & HABITS** Found in forests, gardens and clearings. Occurs in pairs or small bands,

often associating with jays, laughingthrushes and treepies. Wanders a lot in forests, flying across clearings and entering hill-station gardens, one bird following another. Arboreal, but also hunts low in bushes. Even descends to the ground, with long tail cocked as it hops about.

ABOVE: *Red-billed Blue Magpie*

Rufous Treepie ▪ *Dendrocitta vagabunda* 50cm

DESCRIPTION Sexes alike. Rufous above; sooty grey-brown head and neck; black, white and grey on wings, best seen in flight; black-tipped grey tail, long and graduated. **FOOD** Insects, lizards, small birds, eggs, fruits and flower nectar; kitchen scraps in some areas. **VOICE** Common call a fluty, three-note *goo…ge…lay* or *ko…ki…la*; harsh, guttural notes often uttered. **DISTRIBUTION**

Almost all India, to about 1,500m in outer Himalayas. **HABITAT & HABITS** Found in forests, gardens, cultivation and human habitation. Occurs in pairs or small parties; often seen in mixed hunting parties, appearing as leader of pack. Feeds in trees, but also descends low into bushes and on to the ground to pick up termites. Bold and noisy. Rather tame and confiding in certain areas. The **Grey Treepie** *D. formosae* replaces it at higher altitudes.

Grey Treepie

Spotted Nutcracker ▪ *Nucifraga caryocatactes* 32–35cm

DESCRIPTION Chocolate-brown plumage, thickly speckled with white; dark central tail feathers, tipped white; white outer-tail and undertail-coverts; heavy, pointed bill distinctive. Sexes alike. Race *hemispila*, found between Kangra and CE Nepal, has smaller white spots; rump lacks white spots. **FOOD** Mainly ants and large insect larvae, particularly of wood-boring beetles. **VOICE** Noisy; call a guttural *kharr…kharr*. **DISTRIBUTION** Himalayas, 1,800–4,000m, sometimes descending to about 1,200m in winter **HABITAT & HABITS** Found in coniferous, oak and rhododendron forests.

Occurs in small parties. Keeps to treetops but readily descends to the ground. Rather wary. Flies short distances across glades. Quite noisy, usually attracting attention by calls.

Large-billed Crow ■ *Corvus macrorhynchos* 48cm

DESCRIPTION Sexes alike. Glossy black plumage; heavy bill with noticeable culmen-curve.
FOOD Omnivorous. **VOICE** Harsh *khaa...khaa* calls; several variations on this among various
races. **DISTRIBUTION** Subcontinent, to about 4,500m in Himalayas; absent in extreme W
Rajasthan and parts of Punjab. **HABITAT & HABITS** Occurs in forests and rural habitation;
small numbers in towns and cities. Solitary or in groups of 2–6. Most common around villages
and only small numbers in urban areas. Overall not as 'enterprising' as the familiar **House
Crow** C. *splendens*. Behaviour in forested areas often indicates presence of carnivore kills.

Grey-crested Tit ■ *Lophophanes dichrous* 12cm

DESCRIPTION Small, grey and orange tit with dark-edged, whitish moustache extending
around neck as collar. Mottled grey cheeks and throat, and dark recurved eye-stripes.

Underparts pale orange-buff. Sexes alike. **FOOD** Mostly
invertebrates and larvae. **VOICE** Thin *zai* and *ti ti ti ti* calls,
and *chea chea* alarm. Song *wee wee tz tz tz*. **DISTRIBUTION**
Locally common breeding resident in northern mountains

from Kashmir east to
Bhutan. Most common in
east. Winters lower down.
Also China and Myanmar.
HABITAT & HABITS
Inhabits hill forests. Feeds
from middle storeys to the
ground on invertebrates,
often in mixed hunting
groups. Rather quiet and
inconspicuous. Nests in
tree-hole.

Great Tit ■ *Parus major* 13cm

DESCRIPTION Sexes alike. Grey back; black crown continued along sides of neck to broad black band from chin along centre of underbody; white cheeks, nape-patch, wing-bar and outer feathers of black tail; ashy-white sides. The **White-naped Tit** *P. nuchalis* of W India lacks black on neck-sides; has extensive white in wings and sides of body. **FOOD** Insects and small fruits. **VOICE** Loud, clear whistling *whee…chi…chee…*; other whistling and harsh notes. **DISTRIBUTION** Widespread in Himalayas, foothills to about 3,500m; peninsular India from Gujarat, C Rajasthan and Orissa south; absent in broad belt from NW India across Gangetic Plain. **HABITAT & HABITS** Found in open forests, gardens and human habitation. Occurs

in pairs or small bands, often with other small birds. Restless. Clings upside down, and indulges in various acrobatic displays as it hunts among leaves and branches. Holds food fast between feet and pecks at it noisily. Tame and confiding.

Black-lored Tit

■ *Machlolophus xanthogenys* 14cm

DESCRIPTION Large tit with diagnostic bushsy, black crest. Olive back; crest, faintly-tipped yellow; stripe behind eye, broad centeral band from chin to vent; bright yellow nape-patch, supercilium and sides of underbody. Sexes alike. In pairs or small flocks. often with other small birds; arboreal, active; feeds in foliage; sometimes enters gardens. Female and juvenile like male, but may have black replaced by olive. **FOOD** Insects, fruits and seeds. **VOICE** Cheerful, musical notes. Call a loud tailorbird-like *towit…towit* near nest; other 2- to 4-noted whistling calls; whistling song. Also, harsh charrr and some chattering notes. **DISTRIBUTION** The Himalayas to E Nepal; 1,200-2,500 m, widespread in parts of C, E and W India. **HABITAT & HABITS** Inhabits open forest, feeding on invertebrates and seeds at lower levels. Often in mixed hunting groups and a typical tit in behaviour. Nests in tree-holes.

Sultan Tit ▪ *Melanochlora sultanea* 20cm

DESCRIPTION Male: black above; yellow crown and crest; black throat and upper breast; yellow below. Female: deep olivish wash to black upper body and throat; crest as in male; some yellow also on throat. **FOOD** Insects, small fruits and seeds. **VOICE** Noisy; loud, whistling *cheerie…cheerie*; other shrill whistling notes, often mixed with harsh *churr* or

chrrchuk; varied chattering notes. **DISTRIBUTION** Himalayan foothills, east from C Nepal; north-east; foothills to about 1,200m, sometimes ascending to 2,000m. **HABITAT & HABITS** Occupies mixed forests and edges of forest. Occurs in small bands, often with other birds in mixed hunting flocks. Active and inquisitive. Clings sideways and upside down. Checks foliage and bark crevices. Feeds in canopy but also descends to tall bushes.

Rufous-vented Tit ▪ *Periparus rubidiventris* 12cm

DESCRIPTION Very small, plump, dark tit with black throat. Very similar to large **Rufous-naped Tit** *P. rufonuchalis*, but overlapping western race has pinkish-rufous belly (grey in eastern race). Bib much less extensive. Nape all white. Vent always rufous. Sexes

alike. **FOOD** Small invertebrates and larvae, and some seeds. **VOICE** Noisy. Thin *seet* and *psst*. Rattling song. **DISTRIBUTION** Common breeding resident in northern mountains from Himachal Pradesh east to Nagaland. Winters lower down in foothills. Also Tibet, China and Myanmar. **HABITAT & HABITS** Inhabits open coniferous and broadleaved forests, particularly rhododendron. More active when feeding. Will also nest in holes in buildings or trees.

Fire-capped Tit ■ *Cephalopyrus flammiceps* 10cm

DESCRIPTION Tiny, green and yellow tit; male has red crown and throat in breeding plumage. Green above with two thin white wing-bars. Deep yellow below in male, paler in female and almost white in juvenile. Beady black eyes and very short, pointed bill. The **Yellow-browed Tit** *Sylviparus modestus* similar but duller, with stubby bill and faint whitish wing-bars. No red. **FOOD** Small invertebrates, mainly insects; some vegetable material. **VOICE** Soft *tsit* and *tsee tsee tsee*. Song a quiet *we two we-two we two*. **DISTRIBUTION** Local breeding summer visitor to northern mountains from Pakistan east to Arunachal Pradesh. Winters in foothills and rarely in plains south to Maharastra and Madhya Pradesh. Also Tibet, China and Myanmar. **HABITAT & HABITS** Inhabits forest, usually high in canopy but will descend to low growth. Gregarious and joins mixed hunting groups. Easily overlooked.

Black-throated Tit ■ *Aegithalos concinnus* 10.5cm

DESCRIPTION Tiny, chestnut, grey and black tit with white-bordered black throat. Chestnut crown, upper breast and flanks, paler on belly. Broad black stripes through eyes. White irises. Grey upperparts. Tail has white tip and outer feathers. Head pattern distinguishes it from four similar species of Aegithalidae in region. Sexes alike. Juvenile lacks black throat. **FOOD** Insects; fruits. **VOICE** Soft but insistent *trrr trrr* and *chek chek*. **DISTRIBUTION** Common breeding resident in northern mountains from northern Pakistan east to Myanmar border. Moves lower down in foothills in winter. Also China and SE Asia. **HABITAT & HABITS** Inhabits open forest, gardens and forest edges. Very active, confiding and inquisitive. Occurs in small parties, sometimes with mixed hunting groups. Feeds on invertebrates and fruits at all levels. Nests in low bush.

Black-crested Bulbul ■ *Pycnonotus flaviventris* 15cm

DESCRIPTION Sexes alike. Glossy black head, crest and throat; olive-yellow nape and back, becoming brown on tail; yellow below throat. The **Flame-throated Bulbul** *P. m. gularis* of Western Ghats has ruby-red throat. **FOOD** Insects and fruits. **VOICE** Cheerful whistles; also harsh *churr* call; 4–8-note song. **DISTRIBUTION** Himalayas, from Himachal Pradesh eastwards; north-east; foothills to about 2,000m. **HABITAT & HABITS** Inhabits forests, bamboo, clearings and orchards. Occurs in pairs or small bands, sometimes with other birds. Arboreal.

ABOVE: *Flame-throated Bulbul*

Red-whiskered Bulbul
■ *Pycnonotus jocosus* 20cm

DESCRIPTION Sexes alike. Brown above, slightly darker on wings and tail; black perky crest distinctive; crimson 'whiskers' behind eyes; white underbody with broken breast-collar; crimson-scarlet vent. **FOOD** Insects, fruits and flower nectar. **VOICE** Cheerful whistling notes; also harsh, grating alarm notes. **DISTRIBUTION** From Uttarakhand east along Himalayan foothills to about 1,500m; most common south of Satpura mountains in peninsular India; disjunct population in hilly areas of S, SE Rajasthan and Gujarat. **HABITAT & HABITS** Occurs in forests, clearings, gardens, orchards and vicinity of human habitation. Sociable; in pairs or small flocks, or occasionally gatherings of up to 100 birds. Lively and energetic. Feeds in canopy, low bushes and on the ground. Enlivens its surroundings with cheerful whistling notes. Tame and confiding in some areas.

Red-vented Bulbul
■ *Pycnonotus cafer* 20cm

DESCRIPTION Sexes alike. Dark sooty-brown plumage; pale edges of feathers on back and breast give scaly appearance; darker head, with slight crest; almost black on throat; white rump and red vent distinctive; dark tail tipped white. **FOOD** Insects, fruits, flower nectar and kitchen scraps. **VOICE** Cheerful whistling calls; alarm calls on sighting snake, owl or some other intrusion, serving to alert other birds. **DISTRIBUTION** Subcontinent, to about 1,800m in Himalayas. **HABITAT & HABITS** Inhabits light forests, gardens and haunts of man. Occurs in pairs or small flocks, but large numbers gather to feed. Arboreal, keeping to middle levels of trees and bushes. Well-known Indian bird, rather attached to human habitation. Pleasantly noisy and cheerful, lively and quarrelsome. Indulges in dust-bathing. Also hunts flycatcher-style.

Mountain Bulbul
■ *Ixos mcclellandii* 24cm

DESCRIPTION Large, olive and rufous bulbul with shaggy brown crown. Cheeks and breast pale rufous-streaked with buff. Throat streaked white and often puffed out. Belly and vent buff. Upperparts olive-green. Long, powerful bill. Sexes alike. **FOOD** Fruits and insects; possibly also nectar. **VOICE** Noisy, with variety of calls, most commonly metallic *tsyi tsyi* and *cheep har lee*. **DISTRIBUTION** Fairly common breeding resident in northern mountains from Uttaranchal east to Myanmar border and perhaps Bangladesh. Moves lower down to foothills and even adjacent plains in winter. Also SE Asia. **HABITAT & HABITS** Inhabits forest and secondary growth with scattered trees, feeding mainly on fruits, mostly in canopy. Usually in pairs or small groups. Nests high in tree.

Himalayan Bulbul ■ *Pycnonotus leucogenys* 20cm

DESCRIPTION Sexes alike. Brown head, front-pointed crest and short white superciliary stripe. Black around eyes and on chin and throat. **FOOD** Insects, fruits and flower nectar. **VOICE** Pleasant whistling notes. **DISTRIBUTION** Found in Himalayas, from foothills to about 3,400m. **HABITAT & HABITS** Favours open scrub, vicinity of human habitation and edges of forest. Occurs in pairs or small parties. Active birds on the move, attracting attention by its pleasant calls. Himalayan species common in hills, where it is quite confiding.

Black Bulbul ■ *Hypsipetes leucocephalus* 23cm

DESCRIPTION Sexes alike. Ashy-grey plumage; black, loose-looking crest; coral-red

bill and legs diagnostic; whitish below abdomen. **FOOD** Forest berries, fruits, insects and flower nectar. **VOICE** Very noisy; assortment of whistles and screeches. **DISTRIBUTION** Several races; resident in Himalayas and NE India. Southern race *ganeesa* darker, with square tail, and found in Western Ghats and Sri Lanka. **HABITAT & HABITS** Found in tall forests and hill-station gardens. Flocks in forest, often dozens together. Strictly arboreal, keeping to topmost branches of tall forest trees, and rarely coming down into undergrowth. Noisy and restless, hardly staying on a tree for a few minutes. Feeds on berries and other fruits, but also hunts insects in flycatcher manner.

Fire-tailed Myzornis ■ *Myzornis pyrrhoura* 12cm

DESCRIPTION Unmistakable bird; bright, rich, leaf-green above, sometimes washed with gold; slightly paler gold-green below; distinctive black spots on crown; black eye mask; diffused greenish-gold outline around eye mask, on bend of wing; thin, black, slightly downcurved bill; bright red throat and breast; orange-red to centre of underparts below, vent, undertail-coverts; orange-red, white, black wing panels; large white tips to primaries, secondaries; bright red sides to black-tipped tail. Can be spotted solitary, or in small flocks. **FOOD** Insects, spiders and small arthropods, as well as consuming fruit, nectar and sap from trees. **VOICE** Calls include high *tsi…tsi*; rattling *trr…trr*. **DISTRIBUTION** W Nepal eastwards. **HABITAT & HABITS** Dwarf juniper, rhododendron shrubberies; mossy oak, rhododendron forests.

Eurasian Crag Martin ■ *Ptyonoprogne rupestris* 15cm

DESCRIPTION Dusky-brown upperparts and crown; dark brown wings; dark, wedge-shaped tail spotted white on underside; pale chin and throat speckled darker graduating to pale buff-brown on breast and greyish-brown on belly. Pale chevron-shaped scalloping on sides of vent. Sexes similar. Juvenile has lighter throat and indistinct mottling on underparts. Less slender than other species in this family. Feeds close to cliff faces; seen in pairs, or small groups. **FOOD** Insects captured on the wing. **VOICE** Calls include short *plee*, musical *weeeh* and harsh *tshrr*. **DISTRIBUTION** Fairly common but local breeding resident and summer visitor in W Pakistan and N mountains from N Pakistan to Bhutan. Winter visitor to Western Ghats. **HABITAT & HABITS** Rocky gorges, cliffs and old hill forts.

Nepal House Martin ■ *Delichon nipalense* 13cm

DESCRIPTION Dumpy, black and white swallow with white, wrap-around rump. Dark blue-black above. White below. Legs white feathered. Deep tail-fork. The **Asian House**

Martin *D. dasypus* has smaller tail-fork, blackish underwing-coverts, and dingy white rump and vent. Nepal has square tail, dark underwings, and black throat and vent. **FOOD** Winged insects. **VOICE** Noisy. Soft, twittering chirps and short *prrit prrit*. **DISTRIBUTION** Local breeding summer visitor to northern mountains from north Pakistan east to Himachal Pradesh. Scarce passage migrant throughout India, but perhaps overlooked because it flies so high. Some winter in Western Ghats. Also Africa, Europe and mainland Asia. **HABITAT & HABITS** Inhabits mountain valleys with cultivation, cliffs and gorges. Feeds gregariously on aerial insects, often high in the sky. Mixes with swifts and other swallows. Nests colonially against rock faces, under ledges and on outside walls of buildings.

Red-rumped Swallow ■ *Cecropis daurica* 19cm

DESCRIPTION Sexes alike. Glossy steel-blue above; chestnut supercilium, sides of head, neck-collar and rump; dull rufous-white below, streaked brown; deeply forked

tail diagnostic. **FOOD** Insects caught on the wing. **VOICE** Mournful chirping note; pleasant twittering song in breeding male. **DISTRIBUTION** Six races over subcontinent, including Sri Lanka; resident and migratory. **HABITAT & HABITS** Found in cultivation, vicinity of human habitation, town centres and rocky hilly areas. Small parties spend much of the day on the wing. Migrant, winter-visiting race *nipalensis* highly gregarious. Hawks insects with other birds. Perches freely on overhead wires, and thin branches of bushes and trees. Hunts insects in most crowded areas of towns, over markets and refuse heaps, flying with amazing agility, wheeling, banking and stooping with remarkable mastery.

Chestnut-headed Tesia ▪ *Cettia castaneocoronata* 8cm

DESCRIPTION Tiny bird with dumpy body, long legs and stubby tail; olive-green back and chestnut hood; bright lemon-yellow throat and underparts olive-washed yellow; sides of breast and flanks olive-green. **FOOD** Insects and spiders. **VOICE** Chattering *chirruk chirruk…* or loud, piercing *tzit…*, repeated when alarmed. **DISTRIBUTION** Resident in Himalayas and NE Indian hills, to 3,900m. **HABITAT & HABITS** Occurs in thick undergrowth in moist forest, dark ravines near streams, and moss-covered boulders or logs. Shy and elusive. Jerks body when calling. Keeps to the ground, hopping around in bushy undergrowth.

Grey-sided Bush Warbler ▪ *Cettia brunnifrons* 10cm

DESCRIPTION Olive-brown with bright rufous cap; long pale supercilium (well defined in front of eye) with dark eye-stripe; whitish throat and belly with conspicuous grey breast and sides; vent olive-brown. **FOOD** Insects and seeds. **VOICE** Soft *tsik tsik*. **DISTRIBUTION** Altitudinal migrant, breeding to 4,000m in Himalayas; winters below 2,200m. **HABITAT & HABITS** Found in rhododendron shrubberies and bushes at forest edges, open forest and tea gardens in winter. Usually remains close to the ground, feeding in undergrowth. Tail sometimes cocked when disturbed.

Green-crowned Warbler ■ *Phylloscopus burkii* 10cm

DESCRIPTION Sexes alike. Olive-green above; greenish or grey-green eyebrow bordered above with prominent black coronal bands; greenish sides of face, yellow eye-ring; completely yellow below. The **White-spectacled Warbler** *P. intermedius* has grey on crown and whitish eye-ring. **FOOD** Insects. **VOICE** Fairly noisy; sharp *chip…chip…* or *cheup… cheup…* notes. **DISTRIBUTION** Breeds in Himalayas, 2,000–3,000m; winters in foothills, parts of C and E peninsula, Maharashtra, S Madhya Pradesh and NE Andhra Pradesh. **HABITAT & HABITS** Found in forest undergrowth. Occurs in small, restless flocks, often in association with other small birds. Keeps to low bushes and lower branches of trees.

White-spectacled Warbler

Grey-hooded Warbler ■ *Phylloscopus xanthoschistos* 10cm

DESCRIPTION Sexes alike. Grey above; prominent, long white eyebrow; yellowish rump and wings; white in outer tail seen in flight; completely yellow below. The **Grey-cheeked Warbler** *P. poliogenys*, with dark slaty head, white eye-ring, and grey chin and cheeks, is found in Himalayas, east of Nepal. **FOOD** Insects; rarely small berries. **VOICE** Quite vocal; familiar calls in Himalayan forests; loud, high-pitched, double-note call; pleasant, trilling song. **DISTRIBUTION** Himalayas, 900–3,000m; altitudinal movement in winter. **HABITAT & HABITS** Found in Himalayan forests and gardens. Occurs in pairs or small bands, often with mixed hunting parties. Actively hunts and flits in canopy foliage and tall bushes. Highly energetic.

ABOVE: *Grey-cheeked Warbler*

Large-billed Leaf Warbler ■ *Phylloscopus magnirostris* 12cm

DESCRIPTION Sexes alike. Brown-olive above; yellowish supercilium and dark eye-stripe distinctive; 1–2 faint wing-bars, not always easily seen; dull-yellow below. The very similar **Greenish Warbler** *P. trochiloides* (10cm) best identifiable in the field by its call (squeaky, fairly loud *dhciewee* or a *cheee…ee*). **FOOD** Small insects. **VOICE** Distinctive *dir…tee…* call, with first note slightly lower; loud, ringing, five-noted song. **DISTRIBUTION** Breeds in Himalayas, 1,800–3,600m; winters over most of peninsula, though exact range imperfectly known. **HABITAT & HABITS** Occurs in forests and

groves. Usually solitary; sometimes in mixed parties of small birds. Quite active. Spends most time in leafy upper branches of medium-sized trees. Not easy to sight, but characteristic call notes help in confirming presence.

ABOVE: *Greenish Warbler*

Clamorous Reed Warbler ■ *Acrocephalus stentoreus* 19cm

DESCRIPTION Sexes alike. Brown above; distinct pale supercilium; whitish throat, dull buffy-white below; at close range, or in the hand, salmon-coloured inside of mouth visible; calls diagnostic. **FOOD** Insects. **VOICE** Highly vocal; loud *chack, chakrrr* and *khe* notes; distinctive, loud warbling; loud, lively song. **DISTRIBUTION** From Kashmir valley, south through the country. Sporadically breeds in many areas; migrant in others. **HABITAT & HABITS** Reed beds and mangroves. Solitary or in pairs. Difficult to see but easily heard; elusive bird, keeping to dense low reeds, mangroves and low growth, always in and around water. Never associates with other species. Flies low. Immediately vanishes into vegetation; occasionally emerges on reed or bush tops, warbling with throat puffed out.

Booted Warbler
■ *Iduna caligata* 12cm

DESCRIPTION Sexes alike. Dull olive-brown above; short, pale white supercilium; pale buffy-white below. **Blyth's Reed Warbler** *Acrocephalus dumetorum* brighter olive-brown and mostly frequents bushes. **FOOD** Insects. **VOICE** Harsh but low *chak…chak…churrr* calls almost throughout day. Soft, jingling song, sometimes heard before departure in winter grounds. **DISTRIBUTION** Winters over peninsula south from Punjab to W Bengal; breeds in north-west regions, parts of W Punjab. **HABITAT & HABITS** Found in open country with *Acacia* and scrub; occasionally light forests. Solitary or 2–4 birds, sometimes in mixed bands of small birds. Very active and agile, hunting among leaves and upper branches. Overall behaviour very leaf-warbler-like, but calls diagnostic.

Paddyfield Warbler ■ *Acrocephalus agricola* 13cm

DESCRIPTION Sexes alike. Rufescent-brown above; brighter on rump; whitish throat, rich buffy below. **Blyth's Reed Warbler** *A. dumetorum* (14cm) a very common winter visitor; also has whitish throat and buffy under body, but olive-brown upper body is distinctive. **FOOD** Insects. **VOICE** *Chrr…chuck* or single *chack* note, rather harsh in tone. Blyth's has somewhat louder, quicker *tchik…* or *tchi…tchi…* call; rarely, warbling song before migration, around early April. **DISTRIBUTION** Winter visitor; common over most of India, south of and including terai. **HABITAT & HABITS** Found in damp areas, reed growth and tall cultivation. Solitary, hopping in low growth. Rarely seen with other birds. Flies low, but soon vanishes into growth.

ABOVE: *Blyth's Reed Warbler*

Zitting Cisticola ■ *Cisticola juncidis* 10cm

DESCRIPTION Sexes alike. Rufous-brown above, prominently streaked darker; rufous-buff, unstreaked rump; white tips to fan-shaped tail diagnostic; buffy-white underbody, more rufous on flanks. Diagnostic calls. **FOOD** Insects, spiders and possibly some seeds. **VOICE** Sharp, clicking *zit…zit* calls; continuous during display in air. **DISTRIBUTION** Subcontinent, south of Himalayan foothills; absent in extreme NW Rajasthan. **HABITAT & HABITS** Found in open country, grass, cultivation and reed beds; also coastal lagoons. Pairs or several birds occur over open expanse. Great skulker, lurking in low growth. Usually seen during short, jerky flights, low over the ground; soon dives into cover. Most active when breeding, during rains. Male's display striking, involving soaring erratically, falling and rising, and incessantly uttering sharp, creaking note. Adults arrive on nest in similar fashion.

Common Tailorbird ■ *Orthotomus sutorius* 13cm

DESCRIPTION Sexes alike. Olive-green above; rust-red forecrown; buffy-white underbody; dark spot on throat-sides, best seen in calling male; long, pointed tail, often held erect; central tail feathers about 5cm longer and pointed in breeding male. One of India's best-known birds. **FOOD** Insects and flower nectar. **VOICE** Very vocal; loud, familiar *towit…towit*; song a rapid version of call, with slight change, loud *chuvee…chuvee…chuvee*, uttered for up to seven minutes at a stretch; male sings on exposed perch. **DISTRIBUTION** Subcontinent, to about 2,000m in outer Himalayas. **HABITAT & HABITS** Inhabits forest, cultivation and human habitation. Usually in pairs. Rather common in human habitation, but keeps to bushes in gardens. Remains unseen even when at arm's length, but very vocal. Tail often cocked, carried almost to back; clambers up into trees more than other related warblers.

Grey-breasted Prinia ■ *Prinia hodgsonii* 11cm

DESCRIPTION Sexes alike. Grey-brown, with some rufous above; long grey tail, tipped black and white; white underbody; when breeding, soft grey breast-band diagnostic.

FOOD Insects and flower nectar. **VOICE** Noisy when breeding; longish, squeaky song. Contact calls almost continuous squeaking. **DISTRIBUTION** All India south of Himalayan foothills to about 1,800m; absent in arid W Rajasthan. **HABITAT & HABITS** Occupies edges of forests, cultivation, gardens and scrub, often in and around human habitation. Small bands ever on the move. Keeps to low growth but often clambers into middle levels; singing males may climb to tops of trees. Few nearly always present in mixed hunting parties of small birds. Nest like a tailorbird's.

Graceful Prinia ■ *Prinia gracilis* 13cm

DESCRIPTION Sexes alike. Dull grey-brown above, streaked darker; very pale around eyes; long, graduated tail, faintly cross-barred, tipped white; whitish underbody, buffy on belly. Plumage more rufous in winter. The **Striated Prinia** *P. criniger* (16cm) dark brown and streaked. **FOOD** Insects. **VOICE** Longish warble when breeding; male produces wing-snapping and jumping display; *szeep…szip…* call note. **DISTRIBUTION** NW Himalayan foothills, terai, south to Gujarat, across Gangetic Plain. **HABITAT & HABITS** Found in scrub, grass, canal banks and semi-desert. Small parties move in

low growth. Usually does not associate with other birds. Restless, flicking wings and tail often; occasionally hunts like a flycatcher.

Graceful Prinia

Striated Prinia

Plain Prinia ■ *Prinia inornata* 13cm

DESCRIPTION Sexes alike. Pale brown above; whitish supercilium and lores; dark wings and tail; long, graduated tail, with buff tips and white outer feathers; buff-white underbody; tawny flanks and belly. In winter, more rufous above. The **Yellow-bellied Prinia** *P. flaviventris* olivish-green above, with slaty-grey head; yellow belly and whitish throat distinctive. **FOOD** Insects and flower nectar. **VOICE** Plaintive *tee…tee*; also *krrik… krrik* sound; wheezy song, very insect-like in quality. **DISTRIBUTION** Subcontinent, from terai and Gangetic Plain southwards; absent in W Rajasthan. **HABITAT & HABITS** Found in tall cultivation, grass and scrub; prefers damp areas. Pairs or several move about in low growth. Skulker, difficult to see. Jerky, low flight, with bird soon vanishing into bush. Tail often flicked.

Yellow-bellied Prinia

Ashy Prinia ■ *Prinia socialis* 13cm

DESCRIPTION Sexes alike. Rich, ashy-grey above, with rufous wings and long, white-tipped tail; whitish lores; dull buffy-rufous below. In winter less ashy and more rufous-brown; longer tail; whitish chin and throat. **FOOD** Insects and flower nectar. **VOICE** Nasal *pee…pee…pee…*; song a loud, lively *jivee…jivee…jivee…* or *jimmy…jimmy…*, rather like the Common Tailorbird's (p. 97) in quality, but easily identifiable once heard. **DISTRIBUTION** Subcontinent south of Himalayan foothills, to about 1,400m; absent in W Rajasthan. **HABITAT & HABITS** Occurs in cultivation, edges of forest, scrub, parks and vicinity of human habitation. Mostly in pairs. Common and as familiar as the Common Tailorbird in some areas. Actively moves in undergrowth. Often flicks and erects tail. Typical jerky flight when flying from bush to bush. Noisy and excitable when breeding.

Rusty-cheeked Scimitar Babbler ■ *Pomatorhinus erythrogenys* 25cm

DESCRIPTION Sexes alike. Olive-brown above; orangish-rufous (rusty) sides of face, head, thighs and flanks; remainder of underbody mostly pure white; long, curved 'scimitar' bill. **FOOD** Insects, grubs and seeds. **VOICE** Noisy; mellow, fluty whistle, two-noted *cue…pe…cue…pe*, followed by single (sometimes double) note reply by mate. Guttural alarm call and liquid contact note. **DISTRIBUTION** Himalayan foothills to at least 2,200m and possibly 2,600m. **HABITAT & HABITS** Found in forest undergrowth, ravines and bamboo. Occurs in small bands. Bird of undergrowth, hopping on jungle floor. Turns over leaves or digs with bill. Sometimes hops into leafy branches, but more at ease on the ground.

White-browed Scimitar Babbler ■ *Pomatorhinus schistceps* 22cm

DESCRIPTION Largish scimitar babbler with long, broad white supercilium, grey to rufous-brown, even blackish, dark lores, ear coverts. Decurved yellow bill, pale eyes, pure white throat, breast, belly. Chestnut neck-sides, below, breast, flanks; olive-brown upperparts, tail. The similar **Indian Scimitar Babbler** *P. horsfieldii* found in Himalayas. **FOOD** Insects, spiders and flower nectar. **VOICE** often duets hoots, whistles. **DISTRIBUTION** Hilly forest regions of peninsular India, with four races. **HABITAT & HABITS** Dense forest undergrowth; secondary growth. In mixed foraging flocks, with other babblers, bird of mid-storey, hunts in thickets, undergrowth and small tress..

ABOVE: *Indian Scimitar Babbler*

Slender-billed Scimitar Babbler ■ *Pomatorhinus superciliaris* 20cm

DESCRIPTION Sexes alike. Very long, slender, sharply downcurved black bill; relatively small, dark grey head with long white supercilium; dark brown above and brighter rufous-brown below; whitish throat streaked with grey. **FOOD** Insects and berries. **VOICE** Varied calls include series of repeated powerful, mellow hoots uttered rapidly. **DISTRIBUTION** Resident in E Himalayas and NE India. **HABITAT & HABITS** Occurs in moist broadleaved forest and bamboo thickets. Skulking and secretive. Forages in bamboo or low undergrowth. Often in small flocks.

Tawny-bellied Babbler

■ *Dumetia hyperythra* 13cm

DESCRIPTION Sexes alike. Olivish-brown above; reddish-brown front part of crown; white throat in western and southern races; nominate race has entirely fulvous underbody. **FOOD** Mainly insects, but occasionally seen on flowering silk-cotton trees; also other flower nectar. **VOICE** Faint *cheep…cheep* contact notes; also mix of other whistling and chattering notes. **DISTRIBUTION** SE Himachal Pradesh, east along foothills into peninsular India; absent in arid north-west, Punjab plains and extreme north-eastern states. **HABITAT & HABITS** Found in scrub and bamboo, in and around forests. Occurs in small, noisy parties in undergrowth. Rummages on floor, hopping about, always wary. Hardly associates with other birds. Great skulker, difficult to see. At any sign of danger a flock disperses amid a noisy chorus of alarm notes, but soon reunites.

Pin-striped Tit Babbler
■ *Macronus gularis* 11cm

DESCRIPTION Tiny brown babbler with streaked yellowish underparts. Brown above, more olive on mantle and with chestnut crown. Yellowish supercilia and underparts, the latter finely streaked blackish. Pale irises. Sexes alike. **FOOD** Insects, including small caterpillars, ants and grasshoppers; also spiders. **VOICE** Very noisy. Loud, regular, repeated barbet-like *chunk chunk chunk*; also *chrrr*. **DISTRIBUTION** Common breeding resident in northern foothills from Uttaranchal east through Nepal to Arunachal Pradesh, whole of north-east and Eastern Ghats. Also China and SE Asia. **HABITAT & HABITS** Inhabits forest undergrowth and bamboo, often feeding fairly high but also on the ground. Feeds in pairs or small parties, often in mixed hunting groups. Active but furtive. Nests low down.

Puff-throated Babbler
■ *Pellorneum ruficeps* 15cm

DESCRIPTION Sexes alike. Olivish-brown above; dark rufous cap; whitish-buff stripe over eye; white throat; dull fulvous-white underbody, boldly streaked blackish-brown on breast and sides. **FOOD** Insects. **VOICE** Noisy when breeding; mellow whistle, 2–4-noted; best-known call four-note whistle, interpreted as *he-will-beat-you*. **DISTRIBUTION** Hilly forest areas; Himalayas, to about 1,500m, east of SE Himachal Pradesh; north-east states; S Bihar, Orissa, Satpura range across C India, Eastern and Western Ghats. **HABITAT & HABITS** Occupies forest undergrowth, bamboo, overgrown ravines and *nullahs*. Solitary or in pairs. Shy, secretive bird of undergrowth. Mostly heard; very difficult to see. Rummages on the ground, in leaf litter. Hops about, rarely ascending into upper branches.

Common Babbler

■ *Argya caudata* 23cm

DESCRIPTION Sexes alike. Dull brown above, profusely streaked; brown wings; olivish-brown tail long and graduated, cross-rayed darker; dull white throat; pale fulvous underbody, streaked on breast-sides. **FOOD** Insects, flower nectar and berries. **VOICE** Noisy; pleasant, warbling whistles, several birds often in chorus; squeaky alarm notes; calls on the ground and in low flight. **DISTRIBUTION** Most of N, NW, W and peninsular India, south of outer Himalayas to about 2,000m; east to about W Bengal. **HABITAT & HABITS** Found in thorn scrub, open cultivation and grass. Occurs in pairs or small bands in open scrub. Skulker, working its way low in a bush or on the ground; moves with peculiar bouncing hop on the ground, the long, loose-looking tail cocked up. Very wary, vanishing into scrub at slightest alarm. Weak flight, evident when flock moves from one scrub patch to another, in ones and twos.

Striated Babbler

■ *Argya earlei* 21cm

DESCRIPTION Sexes alike. Dull brownish above, streaked darker; long, cross-barred tail; buffy-brown below, with fine dark streaks on throat and breast; the Common Babbler (above) has white throat and lacks breast-streaks. The **Striated Grassbird** *Megalurus plaustris* (25cm), with greatly overlapping range, has bolder streaking above and prominent whitish supercilium, and is almost white below, streaked below breast. **FOOD** Insects and snails. **VOICE** Loud, three-note whistle; also quick-repeated, single whistling note. **DISTRIBUTION** Floodplains of north-east river systems, especially larger rivers. **HABITAT & HABITS** Found in tall grass, reed beds and scrub. Sociable; parties of up to 10 birds keep to tall grass and reed beds. Flies low, rarely dropping to the ground.

Large Grey Babbler ■ *Turdoides malcolmi* 28cm

DESCRIPTION Sexes alike. Grey-brown above; dark centres to feathers on back give streaked look; greyer forehead; long, graduated tail cross-rayed with white outer feathers, conspicuous in flight; fulvous-grey below. **FOOD** Insects, seeds and berries; rarely flower nectar. **VOICE** Very noisy; chorus of squeaking chatter; short alarm note. **DISTRIBUTION** From around E Uttar Pradesh, Delhi environs, south through most of peninsula; east to Bihar; abundant in Deccan. **HABITAT & HABITS** Occupies scrub, open country, gardens and vicinity of human habitation. Gregarious; flocks in open country, sometimes dozens together. Moves on the ground and in medium-sized trees. Hops about, turning over leaves on the ground. Weak flight, never for long. At any sign of danger, a flock comes together.

Spiny Babbler ■ *Turdoides nipalensis* 24cm ℮

DESCRIPTION Upperparts dark rufescent-brown; diagnostic downcurved black bill; white face; pale irises; strong, fine black streaking on throat and breast; tail has narrow, faint cross-bars. **FOOD** Mainly insects, fruits, seeds and beetles.**VOICE** Song a distinctive, harsh, ringing whistling, *ter...ter...ter...ter...ter...ter.* **DISTRIBUTION** Endemic resident in Nepal. **HABITAT & HABITS** Occurs in dense scrub on hillsides; favours thicker areas, away from cultivation. Usually in pairs, feeding on the ground. Shy and difficult to see.

White-crested Laughingthrush ◼ *Garrulax leucolophus* 28cm

DESCRIPTION Sexes alike. Olive-brown above; pure white head, crest, throat, breast and sides of head; broad black band through eye to ear-coverts; rich rufous nuchal collar, continuing around breast; olive-brown below breast. **FOOD** Insects and berries. **VOICE** Very noisy; sudden explosive chatter or 'laughter'; also pleasant two- or three-note whistling calls. **DISTRIBUTION** Himalayas, east of Himachal Pradesh; foothills to 2,400m; most common at 600–1,200m. **HABITAT & HABITS** Found in dense forest undergrowth, bamboo and wooded *nullahs*. Occurs in small parties in forest. Moves in undergrowth but readily ascends into upper leafy branches. Makes short flights between trees. Often seen with other laughingthrushes, treepies and drongos. Hops on the ground, rummaging in leaf litter.

Black-faced Laughingthrush ◼ *Trochalopteron affine* 22cm

DESCRIPTION Sexes alike. Diagnostic blackish face, throat and part of head, and contrasting white malar patches, neck-sides and part of eye-ring; rufous-brown above, finely scalloped on back; olivish-golden flight feathers tipped grey; rufous-brown below throat, marked grey. **FOOD** Insects, berries and seeds. **VOICE** Various high-pitched notes, chuckles; rolling *whirrr* alarm call; four-noted, somewhat plaintive song. **DISTRIBUTION** Himalayas, from W Nepal eastwards; descends to 1,500m in winter. **HABITAT & HABITS** Occupies undergrowth in forest; dwarf vegetation in higher regions. Occurs in pairs or small bands, sometimes with other babblers. Moves on the ground and in low growth; also ascends into middle levels of trees. Noisy when disturbed, or when snakes or other creatures arouse its curiosity.

Variegated Laughingthrush ■ *Trochalopteron variegatum* 28cm

DESCRIPTION Sexes alike. Olive-brown above; grey, black and white head and face; grey, black, white and rufous in wings and tail; black chin and throat, bordered with buffy-white; narrow white tip to tail, with grey subterminal band. **FOOD** Insects and fruits; rarely flower nectar. **VOICE** Noisy; clear, musical whistling notes, 3–4 syllables; also harsh, squeaking notes. **DISTRIBUTION** Himalayas, east to C Nepal; 1,200–3,500m; breeds at 2,000–3,200m. **HABITAT & HABITS** Found in forest undergrowth and bamboo; seen in hill-station gardens in winter. Occurs in small flocks of up to a dozen or more, on steep, bushy hillsides. Keeps to undergrowth for most part, but occasionally clambers into leafy branches. Wary and secretive, and not easily seen. Weak flight, as in most laughingthrushes.

White-throated Laughingthrush ■ *Garrulax albogularis* 28cm

DESCRIPTION Sexes alike. Greyish olive-brown above; fulvous forehead; black mark in front of eye; full, rounded tail with four outer pairs of feathers broadly tipped with white. Rufous below but with conspicuous pure white throat sharply demarcated by line of olive-brown. White gorget stands out in gloom of forest floor. **FOOD** Insects; also berries. **VOICE** Continual chattering; warning *twit-tzee* alarm. **DISTRIBUTION** Throughout Himalayas, with distinct western race *whistleri*, to 3,000m in summer. **HABITAT** Dense forest, scrub and wooded ravines.

Striated Laughingthrush
■ *Grammatoptila striatus* 28cm

DESCRIPTION Sexes alike. Rich-brown plumage, heavily white streaked, except on wings and rich rufous-brown tail; darkish, loose crest, streaked white towards front; heavy streaking on throat and head-sides, becoming less from breast downwards. **FOOD** Insects and fruits; seen eating leaves. **VOICE** Very vocal; clear whistling call of 6–8-notes; loud, cackling chatter. **DISTRIBUTION** 800–2,700m; Himalayas east of Kulu, parts of north-east states. **HABITAT & HABITS** Found in dense forests, scrub and wooded ravines. Occurs in pairs or small parties; often with other birds in mixed, noisy parties. Feeds in upper branches and low bushes. Shows marked preference for certain sites in forest.

Streaked Laughingthrush ■ *Trochalopteron lineatum* 20cm

DESCRIPTION Sexes alike. Pale grey plumage, streaked dark brown on upper back, white on lower back; rufous ear-coverts and wings; rufous edges and grey-white tips to roundish tail; rufous streaking and white shafts on underbody. **FOOD** Insects and berries; refuse around hillside habitation. **VOICE** Fairly noisy; near-constant chatter of mix of whistling and squeaky notes; common call a whistle of 2–3 notes, *pitt…wee…er*. **DISTRIBUTION** Himalayas, west to east; 1,400–3,800m; considerable altitudinal movement. **HABITAT & HABITS** Found in bushy hill slopes, cultivation and edges of forest. Occurs in pairs or small bands. Favours low bush and grassy areas, only rarely going into upper branches. Hops, dips and bows about. Flicks wings and jerks tail often. Weak, short flight.

Red-billed Leiothrix ▪ *Leiothrix lutea* 13cm

DESCRIPTION Male: olive-grey above; dull buffy-yellow lores and eye-ring; yellow, orange, crimson and black in wings; forked tail, with black tip and edges; yellow throat, orange-yellow breast diagnostic; scarlet bill. Red on wing considerably reduced or absent in western race *kumaiensis*. Female: like male, but yellow instead of crimson in wings. **FOOD** Insects and berries. **VOICE** Quite vocal; often utters wistful, piping *tee…tee…tee*;

mix of sudden explosive notes; song a musical warble. **DISTRIBUTION** Himalayas, from Kashmir to extreme north-east; 600–2,700m. **HABITAT & HABITS** Found in forest undergrowth, bushy hillsides and plantations. Occurs in small parties. Often a part of mixed hunting parties of small birds in forest. Rummages in undergrowth but often moves up into leafy branches. Lively, noisy bird.

Rufous Sibia ▪ *Heterophasia capistrata* 20cm

DESCRIPTION Sexes alike. Rich-rufous plumage; grey-brown centre of back (between wings); black crown; slightly bushy crest and sides of head; bluish-grey wings and black

shoulder-patch; grey-tipped long tail; black subterminal tail-band. **FOOD** Insects, flower nectar and berries. **VOICE** Wide range of whistling and sharp notes; rich song of 6–8 syllables in Himalayan summer. **DISTRIBUTION** Himalayas, 1,500–3,000m. Sometimes to about 3,500m; descends to 600m in some winters. **HABITAT & HABITS** Occupies temperate and broadleaved forests. Occurs in small flocks, sometimes with other birds. Active gymnast, ever on the move. Cheerful calls. Hunts in canopy and middle forest levels, moving among moss-covered branches. Springs into the air after winged insects; sometimes hunts like a treecreeper on stems, probing bark crevices.

Nepal Fulvetta ■ *Alcippe nipalensis* 12cm

DESCRIPTION Small, plump, short-billed babbler with white eye-ring. Mainly brown with contrasting grey head and whitish throat to belly. Thin, dark borders to crown-sides. Pale legs. Sexes alike. **FOOD** Insects, berries and nectar. **VOICE** Noisy. Trilling *dzi dzi dzi dzi* and *pi pi pi pi*; also *p p p jet*. **DISTRIBUTION** Locally common breeding resident in northern mountains from W Nepal east to Burmese border and Bangladesh. Moves lower down in winter. Also Myanmar. **HABITAT & HABITS** Inhabits forest undergrowth and middle strata. Feeds inconspicuously on invertebrates, usually in small, active parties. Often acrobatic. Nests low down

White-browed Fulvetta ■ *Fulvetta vinipectus* 11cm

DESCRIPTION Sexes alike. Brown crown and nape; prominent white eyebrow with black or dark brown line above; blackish sides of face; olive-brown above, washed rufous on wings, rump and tail; some grey in wings; whitish throat and breast; olive-brown below. **FOOD** Insects, caterpillars and berries. **VOICE** Fairly sharp *tsuip…* or *tship…* call; also some harsh *chur*ring notes when agitated. **DISTRIBUTION** Himalayas from W Himachal Pradesh; E Himalayas; north-east regions; 1,500–3,500m, over 4,000m in some parts; descends to 1,200m in severe winters. **HABITAT & HABITS** Occurs in scrub in forest, *ringal* bamboo. Up to 20 birds in low growth or lower branches. Energetic and acrobatic. Often seen in mixed hunting parties.

Whiskered Yuhina ■ *Yuhina flavicollis* 13cm

DESCRIPTION Sexes alike. Olive-brown above; chocolate-brown crown and crest; white eye-ring and black moustache seen from close up; rufous-yellow nuchal collar (less distinct in western race *albicollis*); white underbody, streaked rufous-olive on sides of breast and flanks. **FOOD** Insects, berries and flower nectar. **VOICE** Quite vocal; mix of soft, twittering notes and fairly loud, titmice-like 2–3-note call, *chee…chi…chew*. **DISTRIBUTION** Himalayas; W Himachal Pradesh to extreme north-east; 800–3,400m. **HABITAT & HABITS** Found in forests. Occurs in flocks, almost always in association with other small birds. Active and restless, flitting about or hunting flycatcher style. Moves between undergrowth and middle levels of forests, sometimes ascending into canopy. Keeps up a constant twitter.

Oriental White-eye ■ *Zosterops palpebrosus* 10cm

DESCRIPTION Sexes alike. Olive-yellow above; short blackish stripe through eye; white eye-ring distinctive; bright yellow throat and undertail; whitish breast and belly. **FOOD** Insects, flower nectar and berries. **VOICE** Soft, plaintive *tsee…* and *tseer…* notes; short, jingling song. **DISTRIBUTION** All India, from Himalayan foothills to 2,000m; absent

in arid parts of W Rajasthan. **HABITAT & HABITS** Found in forests, gardens, groves and secondary growth. Occurs in small parties of occasionally up to 40 birds, either by itself or in association with other small birds. Keeps to foliage and bushes. Actively moves among leafy branches, clinging sideways and upside down. Checks through leaves and sprigs for insects, and also spends considerable time at flowers. Calls often, both when in branches and when flying in small bands from tree to tree.

Asian Fairy Bluebird ▪ *Irena puella* 28cm

DESCRIPTION Male: glistening blue above; deep velvet-black sides of face, underbody and wings; blue undertail-coverts. Female: verditer-blue plumage; dull black lores and flight feathers. **FOOD** Fruits, insects and flower nectar. **VOICE** Common call a double-noted *wit...weet...*; also *whi...chu...*; some harsh notes occasionally heard. **DISTRIBUTION** Disjunct distribution; one population in Western Ghats and associated hills south of Ratnagiri; another in E Himalayas, east of extreme SE Nepal; Uttarakhand foothills; Andaman and Nicobar Islands. **HABITAT & HABITS** Inhabits dense evergreen forests and *sholas*. Occurs in pairs or small, loose bands. Spends the day in leafy tall branches. Often descends into undergrowth to feed on berries or hunt insects. Calls while flitting among trees. Seen with other birds.

Chestnut-bellied Nuthatch ▪ *Sitta (castanea) cinnamoventris* 12cm

DESCRIPTION Male: blue-grey above; black stripe from lores to nape; whitish cheeks and upper throat; all but central tail feathers black, with white markings; chestnut below. Female: duller chestnut below. Male **White-tailed Nuthatch** *S. himalayensis* has much paler underbody and clear white patch at tail-base. **FOOD** Insects, grubs and seeds. **VOICE** Loud *tzsib...* call; faint twitter; loud whistle during breeding season. **DISTRIBUTION** Lower Himalayas east of Uttarakhand; to about 1,800m; recently split **Indian Nuthatch** *S. castanea* found in peninsula. **HABITAT & HABITS** Found in forests, groves, roadside trees and human habitation. Occurs in pairs or several individuals, often with other small birds. Restless climber; clings to bark and usually works up tree stem, hammering with bill; also moves upside down and sideways. May visit the ground.

White-tailed Nuthatch

Velvet-fronted Nuthatch

■ *Sitta frontalis* 10cm

DESCRIPTION Male: violet-blue above; jet-black forehead; stripe through eye; white chin and throat, merging into vinous-grey below; coral-red bill. Female: lacks black stripe through eye. **FOOD** Insects. **VOICE** Fairly loud, rapidly repeated, sharp, trilling whistles, *chweet… chwit…chwit*. **DISTRIBUTION** From around W Uttarakhand east along lower Himalayas; widespread over hilly, forested areas of C, S and E India; absent in flat and arid regions. **HABITAT & HABITS** Found in forests; also tea and coffee plantations. Pairs or several birds in mixed hunting parties. Creeps about on stems and branches; favours moss-covered trees; also clings upside down, and checks fallen logs and felled branches. Active and agile, quickly moving from tree to tree. Calls often, until long after sunset.

Bar-tailed Treecreeper

■ *Certhia himalayana* 12cm

DESCRIPTION Sexes alike. Streaked blackish-brown, fulvous and grey above; pale supercilium; broad fulvous wing-band; white chin and throat; dull ash-brown below; best recognized by dark brown barring on pointed tail. **FOOD** Insects and spiders. **VOICE** Long-drawn squeak, somewhat ventriloquial. Loud but short, monotonous song; one of the earliest bird songs, heard much before other birds have begun to sing. **DISTRIBUTION** Himalayas, east to W Nepal; from about 1,600m to timberline; descends in winter. **HABITAT & HABITS** Occurs in Himalayan temperate forests. Solitary or several in mixed parties of small birds. Spends almost entire life on tree-trunks; starts climbing from near base, intermittently checking crevices and under moss, and picking out insects with curved bill. Usually climbs to mid-height, then moves to another tree. Sometimes creeps on moss-clothed rocks and walls.

Common Hill Myna ▪ *Gracula religiosa* 28cm

DESCRIPTION Sexes alike. Black plumage with purple-green gloss; white in flight feathers; orange-red bill; orange-yellow legs, facial skin and fleshy wattles on nape and sides of face. **FOOD** Fruits, insects, flower nectar and lizards. **VOICE** Amazing vocalist; great assortment of whistling, warbling and shrieking notes; excellent mimic; much sought-after cage bird. **DISTRIBUTION** Lower Himalaya and terai, from Uttarakhand eastwards. Lesser a bird of Western Ghats, from N Kanara to extreme south, and Sri Lanka; race *peninsularis* restricted to Orissa, E Madhya Pradesh and adjoining Andhra Pradesh. **HABITAT & HABITS** Found in forests and clearings. Small flocks in forest. Very noisy. Mostly arboreal, only occasionally descending into bush or to the ground. Hops among branches and on the ground. Large numbers gather on fruiting trees, with barbets, hornbills and green pigeons. One of the birdwatching spectacles of the Himalayan foothills.

Jungle Myna ▪ *Acridotheres fuscus* 23cm

DESCRIPTION Stocky grey starling with no eye-patches and distinct forehead-tuft. Northern race greyer, southern race browner. Black crown and cheeks, black wings with white patches, and white-tipped black tail. Irises and bill yellow, latter with blue base. Sexes alike. **FOOD** Mainly nectar, fruits including berries, insects and grains; less often human refuse. **VOICE** Noisy. Similar to the Common Hill Myna's (above) but higher with more whistling. **DISTRIBUTION** Locally common breeding resident in northern hills from Pakistan east to Arunachal Pradesh and south through Bangladesh to Orissa, and again down western seaboard from Gujarat to Kerala and W Tamil Nadu. Also SE Asia. **HABITAT & HABITS** Inhabits cultivation, plantations, forest edges, scrub and outskirts of towns and villages. Less associated with humans than Common Hill and Bank Mynas (p. 114) and less confiding. Also less communal except when nesting in colonies in holes in trees, banks or walls.

Bank Myna
■ *Acridotheres ginginianus* 23cm

DESCRIPTION Sexes alike. Bluish-grey neck, mantle and underparts; black head with orange-red wattle around eye; orange-yellow bill; buff-orange tail-tips and wing-patch. **FOOD** Omnivorous; fruits, nectar, insects, kitchen scraps and refuse. **VOICE** Noisy. Call include a great mix of chattering notes. **DISTRIBUTION** Widespread resident in C India. **HABITAT & HABITS** Found in human habitation, cultivation and grassland. Usually in small, scattered groups around human habitation; often along roadside restaurants picking out scraps. Bold and confiding

Common Starling ■ *Sturnus vulgaris* 20cm

DESCRIPTION Glossy black plumage, with iridescent purple and green, and spotted with buff and white; hackled feathers on head, neck and breast; yellowish bill and red-brown legs. Summer (breeding) plumage mostly blackish. Several races winter in India, with head purple or bronze-green, but field identification is not easy in winter. **FOOD** Insects,

berries, grains, earthworms and small lizards. **VOICE** Mix of squeaking, clicking notes; other chuckling calls. **DISTRIBUTION** Race *indicus* breeds in Kashmir to about 2,000m; it and three other races winter over NW and N India, occasionally straying south to Gujarat; quite common in parts of India in winter. **HABITAT & HABITS** Favours meadows, orchards, vicinity of human habitation and open, fallow land. Gregarious, restless bird. Feeds on the ground, moving hurriedly, and digging with bill in soil. Entire flock may often take off from the ground. Flies around erratically or in circles, but soon settles on trees or returns to the ground.

Asian Pied Starling ■ *Gracupica contra* 23cm

DESCRIPTION Sexes alike. Black and white (pied) plumage distinctive; orange-red bill and orbital skin in front of eyes confirm identity. **FOOD** Insects, flower nectar and grains. **VOICE** Noisy; mix of pleasant whistling and screaming notes. **DISTRIBUTION** Bird of N-C, C and E India, south and east of line roughly from E Punjab, through E Rajasthan, W Madhya Pradesh to Krishna delta; escaped cage birds established in several areas outside original range, as in and around Mumbai. **HABITAT & HABITS** Occurs in open cultivation, orchards and vicinity of human habitation. Sociable; small parties move on their own or associate with other birds, notably other mynas and drongos. Common and familiar over its range but keeps a distance from man; may make its ungainly nest in garden trees, but never inside houses, nor does it enter houses. More a bird of open, cultivated areas, preferably where there is water. Attends to grazing cattle. Occasionally raids standing crops.

Chestnut-tailed Starling
■ *Sturnia malabarica* 21cm

DESCRIPTION Sexes alike. Silvery-grey above, with faint brownish wash; dull rufous to breast, brighter below; black and grey in wings. **FOOD** Flower nectar, fruits and insects. **VOICE** Noisy; metallic, whistling call, becoming chatter when there is a flock; warbling song when breeding. **DISTRIBUTION** India, roughly east and south from S Rajasthan to around W Uttarakhand; to about 1,800m in Himalayan foothills. **Blyth's Starling** *S. m. blythii* breeds in SW India, Karnataka and Kerala, spreading north to Maharastra in winter. **HABITAT & HABITS** Occurs in light forest, open country and gardens. Sociable; noisy parties in upper branches of trees, often with other birds. Incessantly squabbles and moves about, indulging in all manner of acrobatic positions to obtain nectar or reach out to fruits. Descends to the ground to pick up insects.

Blyth's Starling

Brahminy Starling ▪ *Sturnia pagodarum* 20cm

DESCRIPTION Sexes alike. Grey, black and rufous myna; black crown, head and crest; grey back; rich buff sides of head, neck and underbody; black wings and brown tail with white sides and tip distinctive in flight. Female has slightly smaller crest, otherwise like male. **FOOD** Fruits, flower nectar and insects. **VOICE** Quite noisy; pleasant mix of chirping notes and whistles, sounding as conversational chatter; good mimic; breeding male has pleasant warbling song. **DISTRIBUTION** Subcontinent, to about 2,000m in W and C Himalayas. **HABITAT & HABITS** Found in light forests, gardens, cultivation and vicinity of human habitation. Occurs in small parties, occasionally collecting into flocks of 20 birds. Associates with other birds on flowering trees or open land. Walks in typical myna style, head held straight up, confident in looks. Communal roosting sites, with other birds.

Rosy Starling ▪ *Pastor roseus* 24cm

DESCRIPTION Sexes alike. Rose-pink and black plumage; glossy black head, crest, neck, throat, upper breast, wings and tail; rest of plumage rose-pink, brighter with approach of spring migration. **FOOD** Grains, insects and flower nectar. **VOICE** Very noisy; mix

of guttural screams, chattering sounds and melodious whistles. **DISTRIBUTION** Winter visitor to India, particularly common in N, W and C India; arrives as early as end of July; most birds depart around mid-April to early May; absent or uncommon east of Bihar. **HABITAT & HABITS** Inhabits open areas, cultivation, orchards and flowering trees around human habitation. Gregarious; flocks often contain young birds (crestless, dull brown and sooty). Often with other mynas on flowering *Erythrina* and *Bombax* trees. Causes damage to standing crops; seen also around grazing cattle and damp open lands. Overall aggressive and very noisy bird. Huge roosting colonies, resulting in deafening clamour before settling.

Long-tailed Thrush ■ *Zoothera dixoni* 27cm

DESCRIPTION Plain olive-brown above; two dull buffy wing-bars and larger wing-patch seen best in flight; buffy throat, breast and flanks, the rest white, boldly spotted dark brown. The confusingly similar **Alpine Thrush** *Z. mollissima* has very indistinct wing-bars; also shorter tail but this characteristic is not very useful in the field. The **Scaly Thrush** *Z. dauma* (26cm) has distinctly spotted back. **FOOD** Insects and snails. **VOICE** Mostly silent; Plain-backed utters loud, rattling alarm note.

DISTRIBUTION Himalayas, east of C Himachal Pradesh; breeds at 2,000–4,000m; descends to about 1,000m in winter. **HABITAT & HABITS** Occurs in timberline forest; scrub in summer; heavy forests in winter. Pairs or several together in winter. Feeds on the ground. Usually difficult to spot until takes off from close by. Flies up into branches if disturbed.

AlpineThrush

Orange-headed Thrush
■ *Geokichla citrina* 21cm

DESCRIPTION Blue-grey above; orangish-rufous head, nape and underbody; white ear-coverts with two dark brown vertical stripes; white throat and shoulder-patch. Orange-headed nominate race has entirely rufous-orange head. **FOOD** Insects, slugs and small fruits. **VOICE** Loud, rich song, often with mix of other birds' calls thrown in; noisy in early mornings and late evenings; also shrill, screechy *kreeee...* call.

DISTRIBUTION Peninsular India south of line from S Gujarat across to Orissa; nominate race breeds in Himalayas, north-east; winters in foothills, terai, parts of E India, Gangetic Plain and south along Eastern Ghats. **HABITAT & HABITS** Occurs in shaded forests, bamboo groves and gardens. Usually in pairs. Feeds on the ground, rummaging in leaf litter and under thick growth. Flies into leafy branch if disturbed. Occasionally associates with laughingthrushes and babblers. Vocal and restless when breeding.

Tickell's Thrush ▪ *Turdus unicolor* 22cm

DESCRIPTION Male: light ashy-grey plumage; duller breast and whiter on belly; rufous underwing-coverts in flight. Female: olive-brown above; white throat, streaked on sides; tawny flanks and white belly. **FOOD** Insects, worms and small fruits. **VOICE** Rich song; double-noted alarm call; also some chattering calls. **DISTRIBUTION** Breeds in Himalayas, 1,500–2,500m, east to C Nepal, and Sikkim; winters along foothills east of Kangra, north-east, and parts of C and E peninsular India. **HABITAT & HABITS** Found in open forests and groves. Occurs in small flocks on the ground, sometimes with other thrushes. Hops fast on the ground, stopping abruptly, as if to check some underground activity. Digs worms from under soil. Flies into trees when approached too close.

Tibetan Blackbird ▪ *Turdus (merula) maximus* 26–29cm

DESCRIPTION Large black bird with long tail without yellow orbital ring. Female even dark brown. Juvenile has rufous-buff underparts with diffuse dark brown barring and

spotting; back and rump variably spotted and barred with rufous-buff; crown and mantle tend to be even dark brown (male) or pale brown (female). **FOOD** Earthworms, molluscs, insects including caterpillars, small lizards and fruits. **VOICE** Call rattling *chak…chak…chak*. Song mournful, repeated whistle, *piew… piew*. **DISTRIBUTION** NW Himalayas. From Uttarakhand east to Arunachal Pradesh in winter. **HABITAT & HABITS** Found in rocky and grassy slopes with dwarf juniper in summer; juniper stands or shrubs in winter. Usually quite wary, but can be confiding. Nests on the ground or in low bushes.

Blue Whistling Thrush ■ *Myophonus caeruleus* 33cm

DESCRIPTION Large, bulky, purple-blue ground thrush with mainly yellow bill. Whole body spangled with lighter, brighter blue. Forehead, shoulders, wing and tail edges bright blue. Sexes alike. Juvenile duller than adults with dusky bill. **FOOD** Insects, crustaceans, amphibians and fruits. **VOICE** Loud, piercing *tzeet* and *zee zeee*. Rambling, whistling song, sounding almost human. **DISTRIBUTION** Common breeding resident in northern mountains from Pakistan east to Myanmar border. Moves lower in winter. Also C and SE Asia, and China. **HABITAT & HABITS** Inhabits damp forests and other wooded areas, usually near water and often in gorges or by road culverts. Perches on stream boulders and low branches. Noisy, bold and usually approachable. Often close to human habitation, even entering buildings. Usually singly or in pairs, feeding on the ground. Nests in rocks, streamside roots or buildings.

White-tailed Rubythroat ■ *Calliope pectoralis* 15cm

DESCRIPTION Male: slaty above; white supercilium; white in tail; scarlet chin and throat; jet-black throat-sides, continuing into broad breast-band; white below, greyer on sides. Female: grey-brown above; white chin and throat; greyish breast. The **Siberian Rubythroat** *C. calliope* male lacks black on breast; has white malar stripe; female has brown breast; winters in NE and E India. **FOOD** Insects and molluscs. **VOICE** Short, metallic call note; short, harsh alarm note; rich, shrill song. **DISTRIBUTION** Breeds in Himalayas, 2,700–4,600m; winters in N, NE India; winter range not properly known. **HABITAT & HABITS** Occurs in dwarf vegetation. Rocky hills in summer. In winter, prefers cultivation, and damp ground with grass and bushes. Solitary; wary and difficult to see. Cocks tail. Hops on the ground, or makes short dashes. Ascends small bush tops.

Siberian Rubythroat

Indian Blue Robin ▪ *Larvivora brunnea* 15cm

DESCRIPTION Male: deep slaty-blue above; white supercilium; blackish lores and cheeks; rich chestnut throat, breast and flanks; white belly-centre and undertail. Female: brown above; white throat and belly; buffy-rufous breast and flanks. The **White-browed Bush Robin** *Tarsiger indicus* male has very long, conspicuous supercilium, and completely rufous-orange underbody; resident in Himalayas. **FOOD** Insects. **VOICE** High-pitched *churr* and harsh *tack*... in winter; breeding male has trilling song, sometimes sung from exposed perch. **DISTRIBUTION** Breeds in Himalayas, 1,500–3,300m. Winters in southern Western Ghats, Ashambu Hills and Sri Lanka. **HABITAT & HABITS** Occurs in dense

rhododendron and *ringal* bamboo undergrowth in summer, and evergreen forest undergrowth and coffee estates in winter. Solitary; rarely in pairs. Great skulker, very difficult to see. Moves in dense growth and hops on the ground. Jerks and flicks tail and wings often.

ABOVE: *White-browed Bush Robin*

Oriental Magpie Robin ▪ *Copsychus saularis* 20cm

DESCRIPTION Male: glossy blue-black and white; white wing-patch and white in outer tail distinctive; glossy blue-black throat and breast; white below. Female: rich slaty-grey,

where male is black. Familiar bird of India. **FOOD** Insects, berries and flower nectar. **VOICE** One of India's finest songsters; rich, clear song of varying notes and tones; male sings from exposed perch, most frequently in March–June, intermittently year round; also has harsh *churr* and *chhekh* notes; plaintive *sweee*... a common call. **DISTRIBUTION** Subcontinent, to about 1,500m in outer Himalayas; absent in extreme W Rajasthan. **HABITAT & HABITS** Occurs in forests, parks and towns. Solitary or in pairs, sometimes with other birds in mixed parties. Hops on the ground, preferring shaded areas. Common around human habitation. When perched, often cocks tail; flicks tail often, especially when making short sallies. Active at dusk.

White-rumped Shama ■ *Copsychus malabaricus* 25cm

DESCRIPTION Male: glossy-black head and back; white rump and sides of graduated tail distinctive; black throat and breast; orange-rufous below. Female: grey where male is black; slightly shorter tail and duller rufous below breast. **FOOD** Insects; rarely flower nectar. **VOICE** Rich songster; melodious, 3–4 whistling notes very characteristic; variety of call notes, including mix of some harsh notes. **DISTRIBUTION** Himalayan foothills, terai, east of Uttarakhand; NE India; hill forests of Bihar, Orissa, SE Madhya Pradesh, E Maharashtra, south along Eastern Ghats to about Cauvery river; entire Western Ghats, from Kerala north to S Gujarat. **HABITAT & HABITS** Inhabits forests, bamboo and hill-station gardens. Usually in pairs. Overall behaviour like Oriental Magpie Robin's (opposite). Arboreal bird, keeping to shaded areas and foliage, and only occasionally emerging in open. Launches short sallies and hunts until late in evening.

Indian Robin ■ *Saxicoloides fulicatus* 16cm

DESCRIPTION Several races in India. Males differ in having dark brown, blackish-brown or glossy blue-back upper body. Male: dark brown above; white wing-patch; glossy blue-black below; chestnut vent and undertail. Female: lacks white in wings; duller grey-brown below. **FOOD** Insects. **VOICE** Long-drawn *sweeeech* or *weeeech* call; warbling song when breeding; also guttural *charrr...* note. **DISTRIBUTION** Subcontinent, south of Himalayan foothills; absent extreme north-east. **HABITAT & HABITS** Occurs in open country, edges of forest, vicinity of human habitation and scrub. Solitary or in pairs; rather suspicious and maintains safe distance from humans. Hunts on the ground, hopping or running in short spurts. When on the ground, holds head high and often cocks tail right up to back, flashing chestnut vent and undertail.

Black Redstart
■ *Phoenicurus ochruros* 15cm

DESCRIPTION Male: black above (marked with grey in winter); grey crown and lower back; rufous rump and tail-sides; black throat and breast; rufous below. Female: dull brown above; tail as male's; dull tawny-brown below. Eastern race *rufiventris* has black crown, and is the common wintering bird of India. **FOOD** Insects, mostly taken on the ground. **VOICE** Squeaking *tictititic…* call, often beginning with faint *tsip…* note; breeding male has trilling song. **DISTRIBUTION** Breeds in Himalayas, 2,400–5,200m; winters over much of subcontinent. **HABITAT & HABITS** Occurs in open country and cultivation. Mostly solitary in winter, when common all over India. Easy bird to see, in winter and in its open high-altitude summer country. Perches on overhead wires, poles, rocks and stumps. Characteristic shivering of tail and jerky body movements. Makes short dashes to the ground, soon returning to perch with catch. Rather confiding in summer, breeding in houses, under roofs and in wall crevices.

Blue-fronted Redstart ■ *Phoenicurus frontalis* 15cm

DESCRIPTION Male: bright blue forehead with darker blue crown and back; orange-chestnut underparts; rufous rump; orange tail with broad blackish terminal band and central feathers. Female: dark olive-brown; yellowish-orange below; rump and tail as in male; tail pattern diagnostic, separating it from other female redstarts. **FOOD** Insects, seeds and berries. **VOICE** Squeaking *tik* or *prik*. **DISTRIBUTION** Altitudinal migrant; breeds in Himalayas to 5,300m; winters in Himalayan foothills. **HABITAT & HABITS** Occurs in cultivation, open country and gardens. Mostly solitary, perching on rocks or bushes. Drops to the ground to feed. Pumps tail.

Plumbeous Water Redstart ■ *Phoenicurus fuliginosus* 12cm

DESCRIPTION Male: slaty-blue plumage; chestnut tail diagnostic; rufous on lower belly. Female: darkish blue-grey-brown above; two spotted wing-bars; white in tail; whitish below, profusely mottled slaty. Young birds brown, also with white in tail. **FOOD** Insects and worms. **VOICE** Sharp *kreee…* call; also snapping *tzit…tzit*; breeding male has rich, jingling song, infrequently uttered in winter. **DISTRIBUTION** Himalayas, 800–4,000m, but mostly 1,000–2,800m; also breeds south of Brahmaputra river; in winter may descend into foothills and terai. **HABITAT & HABITS** Occurs around mountain streams, rivers and rushing torrents. Pairs on mountain rivers. Active birds, making short dashes from boulders; moves from boulder to boulder, flying low over roaring waters. Tail often fanned open and wagged. Hunts late in evening. Maintains feeding territories in winter and at other times.

White-capped Water Redstart ■ *Phoenicurus leucocephalus* 19cm

DESCRIPTION Sexes alike. Black back, head-sides, wings and breast; white crown diagnostic; chestnut rump and tail; black terminal tail-band; chestnut below breast. **FOOD** Insects. **VOICE** Loud, plaintive *tseeee* call; also *psit…psit…* call; breeding male has whistling song. **DISTRIBUTION** Himalayas: 2,000–5,000m; descends into foothills in winter. **HABITAT & HABITS** Occurs around rocky streams; also on canals in winter. Solitary or pairs on Himalayan torrents; rests on rocks amid gushing waters, flying very low over water to catch insects. Jerks and wags tail and dips body. Restless bird. Courting male has interesting display.

Little Forktail ▪ *Enicurus scouleri* 12cm

DESCRIPTION Sexes alike. Black and white plumage. Black above, with white forehead; white band in wings extends across lower back; small black rump-patch; slightly forked,

short tail with white in outer feathers; black throat, white below. **FOOD** Aquatic insects. **VOICE** Rather silent except for rarely uttered sharp *tzittzit* call. **DISTRIBUTION** Himalayas, west to east. Breeds at 1,200–3,700m; descends to about 300m in winter. **HABITAT & HABITS** Occurs around rocky mountain streams and waterfalls. Solitary or in pairs; bird of mountain streams, waterfalls and small, shaded forest puddles. Moves energetically on moss-covered, wet, slippery rocks. Constantly wags and flicks tail. Occasionally launches short sallies, but also plunges underwater, dipper style.

Spotted Forktail ▪ *Enicurus maculatus* 25cm

DESCRIPTION Sexes alike. White forehead and forecrown; black crown and nape; black back spotted white; broad white wing-bar and rump; deeply forked, graduated,

black and white tail; black to breast, white below. White-spotted back easily distinguishes it from other similar sized forktails in Himalayas. **FOOD** Aquatic insects and molluscs. **VOICE** Shrill, screechy *kree* call, mostly in flight; also some shrill, squeaky notes on perch. **DISTRIBUTION** Himalayas; breeds mostly at 1,200–3,600m; descends to about 600m in winter. **HABITAT & HABITS** Occurs around boulder-strewn torrents, forest streams and roadsides. Solitary or in scattered pairs. Active bird, moving on mossy boulders at water's edge or in mid-stream. Long, forked tail gracefully swayed, and almost always kept horizontal. Flies low over streams, calling. Sometimes rests in shade of forest. Commonly seen in Himalayas.

Common Stonechat
▪ *Saxicola torquatus* 13cm

DESCRIPTION Male: black above; white rump, wing-patch and sides of neck/breast (collar); black throat; orange-rufous breast. In winter, black feathers broadly edged buff-rufous-brown. Female: rufous-brown above, streaked darker; unmarked yellowish-brown below; white wing-patch and rufous rump. **FOOD** Insects. **VOICE** Double-noted *wheet chat* call; soft, trilling song of breeding male in Himalayas, occasionally in winter grounds. **DISTRIBUTION** Breeds in Himalayas, 1,500–3,000m; winters all India except Kerala and much of Tamil Nadu. **HABITAT & HABITS** Occurs in dry, open areas, cultivation and tidal creeks. Solitary or in pairs in open country. Perches on small bush tops, fence-posts and boulders. Restless; makes short trips to the ground to capture insects, soon returning to perch.

Pied Bushchat ▪ *Saxicola caprata* 13cm

DESCRIPTION Male: black plumage; white in wing, rump and belly. Female: brown above, paler on lores; darker tail; dull yellow-brown below, with rusty wash on breast and belly. **FOOD** Insects. **VOICE** Harsh, double-noted call serves as contact and alarm call; breeding male has short, trilling song. **DISTRIBUTION** Subcontinent, from outer Himalayas to about 1,500m. **HABITAT & HABITS** Occurs in open country, scrub, cultivation and ravines. Solitary or in pairs; perches on bush, overhead wire, pole or earth mound. Makes short sallies on to the ground, either devouring prey there or carrying it to perch. Active. Sometimes guards feeding territories in winter. Flicks and spreads wings. Male has fascinating courting display flight (April–May).

Grey Bushchat ■ *Saxicola ferreus* 15cm

DESCRIPTION Male: dark grey above, streaked black; black mask; white supercilium, wing-patch and outer tail; white throat and belly; dull grey breast. Female: rufous-brown, streaked; rusty rump and outer tail;

white throat; yellow-brown below. **FOOD** Insects. **VOICE** Double-noted call; also grating *praee...* call; trilling song of male. **DISTRIBUTION** Himalayas, 1,400–3,500m; descends into foothills and adjoining plains, including Gangetic Plain, in winter. **HABITAT & HABITS** Occurs in open scrub, forest edges and cultivation. Solitary or in pairs; like other chats, keeps to open country and edges of forest. Perches on bush tops and poles, flirting tail often. Regularly seen in an area. Flies to the ground on spotting insect.

Desert Wheatear ■ *Oenanthe deserti* 15cm

DESCRIPTION Male: sandy above, with whitish rump and black tail; black wings; white in coverts; black throat and head-sides; creamy-white below. Female: brown wings and tail; lacks black throat. Winter male: throat feathers fringed white. The **Isabelline Wheatear** *O. isabellina* (16cm) larger and sandy-grey, without black throat. Male **Northern Wheatear** *O. oenanthe* grey above, with white rump and tail-sides, black tail-centre and tip like inverted 'T'; black ear-coverts and wings. **FOOD** Insects. **VOICE** In winter occasional *ch... chett* alarm note; reportedly utters short, plaintive song in winter. **DISTRIBUTION** Winter visitor over N, C and W India, almost absent south of S Maharashtra and Andhra Pradesh; Tibetan race *oreophila* breeds in Kashmir, Ladakh, Lahaul and Spiti, at about 3,000–5,000m. **HABITAT & HABITS** Occurs in open, rocky, barren country; sandy areas; fallow lands. Keeps to the ground or perches on low bush or small rock. Has favoured haunts. Colouration makes it difficult to spot. Makes short sallies to capture insects.

Isabelline Wheatear   *Northern Wheatear*

Grandala ■ *Grandala coelicolor* 23cm

DESCRIPTION Large, purplish-blue, thrush-like chat of high mountains. Male all-shining purplish-blue with blackish wings and tail. Much brighter than similar sized Blue Rock Thrush (p. 127). Female and immature white-streaked brownish-grey with white patches on wings and bluish wash on rump. **FOOD** Insects, fruits including berries, and seeds. **VOICE** Sharp *jeeu jeeu*. Song an extension of this. **DISTRIBUTION** Locally common breeding resident of high mountains from Kashmir east to Arunachal Pradesh. Descends a little lower in winter but always remains in mountain zone. Also Tibet, China and Myanmar. **HABITAT & HABITS** Inhabits rocky hillsides and pastures above treeline. Usually in (often large) flocks, catching invertebrates on the wing or on the ground. Flocks often feed wheeling high in sky like starlings. Perches upright on rocks and hops on the ground. Rarely descends below treeline. Nests on rock ledges.

Blue Rock Thrush ■ *Monticola solitarius* 23cm

DESCRIPTION Male: blue plumage; brown wings and tail; pale fulvous and black scales most conspicuous in winter; belly whiter in winter. Female: duller, grey-brown above; dark shaft-streaks; black barring on rump; dull white below, barred brown. **FOOD** Insects and berries; rarely flower nectar. **VOICE** Silent in winter; breeding male utters short, whistling song. **DISTRIBUTION** Breeds in Himalayas, from extreme west to E Nepal; 1,200–3,000m, perhaps higher; winters from foothills, north-east, south throughout peninsula; uncommon in Gangetic Plain. **HABITAT & HABITS** Inhabits open, rocky country, cliffs, ravines, ruins and human habitation. Solitary; has favoured sites, often around human habitation. Perches on rocks, stumps and roof tops. Rather upright posture. Flies to the ground to feed, but sometimes launches short aerial sallies.

Chestnut-bellied Rock Thrush ■ *Monticola rufiventris* 23cm

DESCRIPTION Male: cobalt-blue head and upperparts with blackish mask; rich chestnut belly. Female: olive-brown with buff throat and lores; heavy scaling on underparts; distinctive face pattern with eye-ring, dark malar stripe and neck-patch. **FOOD** Insects and berries. **VOICE** Harsh rattle; fluty song. **DISTRIBUTION** Himalayan forests to 3,500m. **HABITAT & HABITS** Occurs in open country, forest edges and groves on rocky hillsides. Mostly solitary or seen in pairs. Perches upright.

Blue-capped Rock Thrush
■ *Monticola cinclorhynchus* 17cm

DESCRIPTION Male: blue crown and nape; black back; broad stripe through eyes to ear-coverts; blue throat and shoulder-patch; white wing-patch and chestnut rump distinctive; chestnut below throat. Back feathers edged fulvous in winter. Female: unmarked olive-brown above; buffy-white below, thickly speckled with dark brown. Female Blue Rock Thrush (p. 127) grey-brown above, with yellow-brown vent and dull wing-bar. **FOOD** Insects, flower nectar and berries. **VOICE** Mostly silent in winter, except for occasional harsh, single or double-noted call; breeding male has rich song. **DISTRIBUTION** Breeds in Himalayas, 1,000–2,500m, sometimes higher; winters in Western Ghats, from Narmada river south; sporadic winter records from C Indian forests. **HABITAT & HABITS** Occurs in shaded forests and groves. Solitary or in pairs. Elusive forest bird. Moves in foliage in mixed parties or rummages on the ground in leaf litter. Best seen emerging in clearing.

Asian Brown Flycatcher ■ *Muscicapa dauurica* 13cm

DESCRIPTION Sexes alike; ashy-brown; greyish wash on dirty white breast; short tail; large head with huge eye and prominent eye-ring; basal half of lower mandible pale and fleshy; black legs. The **Brown-breasted Flycatcher** M. *muttui* similar but has pronounced brown breast-band, and larger bill with entirely pale lower mandible. **FOOD** Insects. **VOICE** Call a thin *tzee*; whistling song. **DISTRIBUTION** Breeding resident of Himalayan foothills, with several small disjunct populations resident in hills of central and peninsular India; widespread winter visitor in peninsula. **HABITAT & HABITS** Occurs in open forest, groves, gardens and plantations. Usually solitary. Perches upright on lower branches of trees, making sallies to catch insects and returning to same perch.

Brown-breasted Flycatcher

Rufous-gorgeted Flycatcher ■ *Ficedula strophiata* 14cm

DESCRIPTION Male: dark olive-brown upperparts; blackish face and throat; conspicuous white forehead and eyebrow; diagnostic rufous-orange gorget that is not always visible; grey breast; white sides to black tail. Female: similar but duller, with less distinct eyebrow and gorget. **FOOD** Insects. **VOICE** Metallic *pink*, harsh *trrt*. **DISTRIBUTION** Uncommon resident in Himalayas and NE Indian hills. **HABITAT & HABITS** Inhabits forest clearings and edges. Often seen perched quietly in shaded areas or dense canopy. Like all flycatchers, hawks insects but sometimes feeds on the ground.

Ultramarine Flycatcher ■ *Ficedula superciliaris* 10cm

DESCRIPTION Male: deep blue above and sides of head, neck and breast, forming broken breast-band; long white eyebrow; white in tail; white below. Female: dull-slaty above; grey-white below. Eastern race *aestigma* lacks white over eye and in tail. **FOOD** Insects. **VOICE** Faint *tick… tick…* in winter; *chrrr* alarm note; three-syllable song in Himalayas. **DISTRIBUTION** Breeds in Himalayas, 1,800–3,200m; winters in C India, south to Karnataka and Andhra Pradesh. **HABITAT & HABITS** Inhabits

forests, groves, orchards and gardens. Solitary or in pairs; seen in mixed parties during winter. Active. Hunts in characteristic flycatcher style. Rarely ventures into open.

Slaty-blue Flycatcher ■ *Ficedula tricolor* 13cm

DESCRIPTION Slim, long-tailed flycatcher. Male: slaty-blue above; greyish-white (Himalayas) or buff (S Assam hills) below; black mask; white patch at base of black tail. Female: brown upperparts; warm brownish-buff flanks; rufescent rump and tail. **FOOD** Insects. **VOICE** Faint *tick tick* call. **DISTRIBUTION** Breeds in Himalayas at 1,800–2,600m; winters in foothills. **HABITAT & HABITS** Occupies forest undergrowth, reeds, bushes and grass. Usually solitary or in pairs. Feeds near the ground with tail cocked.

Little Pied Flycatcher ▪ *Ficedula westermanni* 11cm

DESCRIPTION Small, stocky, black and white flycatcher with large head. Small black bill. Male black above with broad white stripes on head, wings and tail-sides, and white underparts. Female and juvenile warm brown above with thin buff wing-bar, rusty rump, white throat and buffish underparts; very similar to female Slaty-blue Flycatcher (opposite), which lacks wing-bar. **FOOD** Small invertebrates and larvae, principally flies, beetles and weevils. **VOICE** Rather silent. Mellow *tweet* and thin, high song. **DISTRIBUTION** Locally common breeding resident and altitudinal migrant in Himalayas from Himachal Pradesh to Myanmar border. Winters in foothills and, more rarely, eastern plains south to southern peninsula. Also China and SE Asia. **HABITAT & HABITS** Inhabits tree canopies in forests and open wooded areas. Occurs singly or in pairs and often with mixed hunting groups. Feeds very actively on insects in leaves and on bark. Nests on the ground, usually on banks.

Verditer Flycatcher ▪ *Eumyias thalassinus* 15cm

DESCRIPTION Male: verditer-blue plumage, darker in wings and tail; black lores. Female: duller, more grey overall. The **Pale Blue Flycatcher** *Cyornis unicolor* (16cm) male uniform blue, with white on belly; female olive-brown. **FOOD** Insects. **VOICE** Silent in winter, except for rare, faint *chwe…* call; rich, trilling notes and song during Himalayan summer. **DISTRIBUTION** Breeds in Himalayas; 1,200–3,200m; winters in Indian plains and hill forests of C, E and S India. **HABITAT & HABITS** Occurs in open forests and orchards. Solitary or in pairs in winter, sometimes with other birds. Restless, flicking tail. Swoops about, ever on the move, occasionally descending quite low. More noticeable than other flycatchers because of its continuous movement and habit of perching in open, exposed positions, like a bare twig on a treetop.

Pale Blue Flycatcher

Verditer Flycatcher

Tickell's Blue Flycatcher
▪ *Cyornis tickelliae* 14cm

DESCRIPTION Male: dark indigo-blue above; bright blue on forehead and supercilium; darker, almost appearing black, on face-sides; rufous-orange throat and breast; whitish below. Female: duller overall. **FOOD** Insects. **VOICE** Clear, metallic song of six notes, sometimes extending to 9–10; often uttered in winter. **DISTRIBUTION** All India, south roughly of line from Kutch to W Uttarakhand east along terai; absent in extreme N, NW India. **HABITAT & HABITS** Occupies shaded forests, bamboo and gardens. Usually in pairs in shaded areas, often in mixed hunting parties. Favours vicinity of wooded streams. Flits about intermittently or launches short sorties. Has favourite perches. Often breaks into fluty song.

Small Niltava ▪ *Niltava macgrigoriae* 13cm

DESCRIPTION Very small, dark blue flycatcher. Male identical to, but much smaller than, the **Large Niltava** N. *grandis* except lower breast and belly are paler greyish-blue, palest in western populations. Female also similar to Large but paler buff on belly. Blue neck-patches often difficult to see. **FOOD** Insects and berries. **VOICE** High-pitched, undulating *twee twee it twee*. Also *churrs*. **DISTRIBUTION** Fairly common endemic breeding resident of northern mountains from Uttaranchal east to Myanmar border. Moves lower down in winter. **HABITAT & HABITS** Inhabits shady shrubberies and understoreys of damp forests, often along streams or in ravines; also grass jungle in winter. Active but often skulking and difficult to see well. Feeds on insects in air and on the ground. Usually occurs singly or in pairs. Nests near the ground.

Rufous-bellied Niltava
◼ *Niltava sundara* 15cm

DESCRIPTION Blue patch on neck-sides.
Male: deep purple-blue back and throat; dark
blue mask; black forehead; brilliant blue crown,
shoulders and rump; chestnut-rufous underbody.
Female: olivish-brown overall; rufescent tail;
white on lower throat diagnostic. The **Large
Niltava** *N. grandis* (21cm) male dark blue
with tufted forehead. The **Blue-throated Blue
Flycatcher** *Cyornis rubeculoides* male has dark
blue throat and white belly; duller, uniform
blue above. **FOOD** Insects. **VOICE** Squeaky
churring note; occasionally sharp *psi…psi*; also
some harsh notes and squeaks. **DISTRIBUTION**
Himalayas, north-east; 1,500–3,200m; winters
in foothills and adjoining plains. **HABITAT &
HABITS** Occurs in dense forest undergrowth
and bushes. Mostly solitary. Keeps to
undergrowth. Highly unobtrusive; seldom seen.
Often flicks wings like a redstart, and bobs body.

Blue-throated Blue Flycatcher   *Large Niltava*

Golden-fronted Leafbird ◼ *Chloropsis aurifrons* 19cm

DESCRIPTION Leaf-green plumage; golden-orange forehead; blue shoulder-patches; dark
blue chin (blackish in southern races) and cheeks; black lores and ear-coverts, continuing
as loop around blue throat. **FOOD** Insects, spiders and flower nectar. **VOICE** Noisy;
wide assortment of whistling notes,
including imitations of several species;
most common call drongo- or shikra-
like *che…chwe*. **DISTRIBUTION**
To about 1,600m in Uttarakhand
Himalayas; east to Bihar, Orissa, south
along Eastern Ghats and up Western
Ghats and adjoining areas. **HABITAT
& HABITS** Inhabits forests. Pairs occur
in leafy canopy. Lively bird, actively
hunting in foliage. Wide range of
whistling and harsh notes immediately
attract attention. Due to greenish
plumage, difficult bird to see in foliage.
Rather aggressive, driving away other
birds, especially on flowering trees.

Thick-billed Flowerpecker
■ *Dicaeum agile* 9cm

DESCRIPTION Sexes alike. Olive-grey above, greener on rump; white-tipped tail; dull whitish-grey below, streaked brown, more on breast; orange-red eyes and thick, blue-grey bill seen at close range. **FOOD** Figs, and berries of *Ficus*, *Lantana*, *Loranthus* and *Viscum*; also insects, spiders and nectar. **VOICE** Loud, sharp *chik…chik*. **DISTRIBUTION** India south of and including Himalayan foothills; absent over arid parts of NW India and from large tracts of Tamil Nadu. **HABITAT & HABITS** Found in forests, orchards and gardens. Solitary or in pairs in canopy foliage. Arboreal, restless. Flicks tail often as it hunts under leaves or along branches; frequents parasitic clumps of *Loranthus* and *Viscum*.

Pale-billed Flowerpecker ■ *Dicaeum erythrorhynchos* 8cm

DESCRIPTION Sexes alike. Olive-brown above; unmarked grey-white below; pinkish-flesh and yellow-brown bill seen only at close range or in good light. The **Nilgiri Flowerpecker** *D. concolor* has dark bill and pale supercilium. **FOOD** Causes damage to orchards, especially mango and guava; chiefly berries, spiders and small insects. **VOICE** Sharp, loud *chik…chik*. **DISTRIBUTION** From Kangra east along foothills to NE India; peninsular India south of line from W Gujarat to S Bihar. **HABITAT & HABITS** Occurs in light forests and groves. Solitary or 2–3 birds in canopy. Frequents parasitic *Loranthus* and *Viscum*. Flits from clump to clump. Strictly arboreal, restless. Territorial even when feeding.

ABOVE: *Nilgiri Flowerpecker*

Fire-breasted Flowerpecker ■ *Dicaeum ignipectus* 7cm

DESCRIPTION Male: metallic blue-green-black above; buffy below, with scarlet breast-patch and black stripe down centre of lower breast and belly. Female: olive-green above, yellowish on rump; bright buff below; flanks and sides tinged olive. **FOOD** Berries, nectar, spiders and small insects. **VOICE** Sharp, metallic *chip…chip* note; high-pitched, clicking song. **DISTRIBUTION** Himalayas, Kashmir to extreme east; breeds at 1,400–3,000m; winters as low as 300m. **HABITAT & HABITS** Occurs in forests and orchards. Mostly solitary. Arboreal and active. Flits about in foliage canopy, attending *Loranthus* clumps. May be seen in restless mixed hunting bands of small birds in Himalayan forests.

Scarlet-backed Flowerpecker ■ *Dicaeum cruentatum* 7cm

DESCRIPTION Very small flowerpecker; bright red from crown to back. Black head-sides; black cheeks; glossy blue-black upperwing; short black tail. Greyish-white underparts; darker grey flanks. Longish, slender bill. Female brownish above and buff below, with red rump and black tail. Juvenile has hint of red on uppertail-coverts and red bill. **FOOD** Fruits, nectar, figs, mistletoes and insects. **VOICE** Noisy. Penetrating *chip…chip* call; repeated *tissit…tissit* song. **DISTRIBUTION** Scarce breeding resident in hills from E Nepal (where rare), NE India and Bangladesh. **HABITAT & HABITS** Occurs in open forests, secondary growth and orchards, wherever there is *Loranthus*. Usually solitary, in pairs or in small parties. Noisily flies from clump to clump high in canopy. Pouch-shaped nest high in trees.

Purple Sunbird ■ *Cinnyris asiaticus* 10cm

DESCRIPTION Breeding male: metallic purple-blue above, and on throat and breast; dark purplish-black belly; narrow chestnut-maroon band between breast and belly; yellow and scarlet pectoral tufts, normally hidden under wings. Female: olive-brown above; pale yellow below (*zeylonica* female has whitish throat). Non-breeding male: much like female but with broad purple-black stripe down centre of throat to belly. **FOOD** Nectar, small insects and spiders. **VOICE** More noisy than other sunbirds; loud *chweet...* notes. **DISTRIBUTION** Subcontinent, south from Himalayan foothills to about 1,500m. **HABITAT & HABITS** Occurs in open forests, gardens and groves. Solitary or in pairs. Important pollinating agent, almost always seen around flowering trees and bushes. Displays amazing agility and acrobatic prowess when feeding. Sometimes hunts flycatcher style.

Gould's Sunbird ■ *Aethopyga gouldiae* 10cm

DESCRIPTION Male: Strikingly coloured with rich red mantle and back; bright yellow underparts; purplish-blue crown and throat; metallic-blue tail; yellow rump. Female: olive-brown with yellow belly, vent and rump-band; grey crown and throat. **FOOD** Nectar. **VOICE** Sharp *tzit-tzit*. **DISTRIBUTION** Resident in Himalayas and NE Indian hills. **HABITAT & HABITS** Occurs in rhododendrons, forest, gardens and scrub. Mostly solitary; sometimes in groups with Green-tailed Sunbird (opposite).

Green-tailed Sunbird ■ *Aethopyga nipalensis* 11cm

DESCRIPTION Male: dark metallic blue-green head and nape, bordered by maroon
mantle; olive-green back and wings;
metallic blue-green tail (appears
dark); underparts bright yellow with
red-streaked breast; yellow rump not
always visible. NW Himalayan race
horsfieldi has less maroon on mantle.
Female: olive-green with greyish-olive
throat; yellowish-olive on belly; rump
slightly yellower than upperparts; pale
tips to tail. **FOOD** Nectar. **VOICE**
Sharp *zig-zig*. **DISTRIBUTION**
Resident in Himalayas. **HABITAT**
Oak and rhododendron forests, scrub
and gardens.

Crimson Sunbird ■ *Aethopyga siparaja* 15cm

DESCRIPTION Male: long tail; metallic-green crown and tail; deep crimson back and
neck-sides; yellow rump not commonly seen; bright scarlet chin and breast; olive-yellow
belly. Female: olive plumage, yellower below. In Western Ghats **Vigor's Sunbird** A. s.
vigorsii, male's breast streaked yellow. **FOOD** Nectar, small insects and spiders. **VOICE**
Sharp, clicking call notes; breeding male utters pleasant chirping song (June–August).
DISTRIBUTION Resident in Himalayas and hills of NE India; winters in Himalayan
plains. **HABITAT & HABITS** Occurs in forests and gardens. Solitary or in pairs. Active
gymnast, hanging upside down and sideways as it probes flowers; also hovers. Moves a lot
in forest, between tall bushes and canopy.

ABOVE: *Vigor's Sunbird*

Little Spiderhunter
■ *Arachnothera longirostra* 14cm

DESCRIPTION Sexes alike. Olive-green above; dark tail, tipped white; grey-white throat, merging into yellow-white below; orangish pectoral tufts. Very long, curved bill diagnostic. Much larger **Streaked Spiderhunter** *A. magna* (17cm) olive-yellow, profusely streaked. **FOOD** Nectar; also insects and spiders. **VOICE** High-pitched *chee…chee* call; loud *which… which…* song, sounding somewhat like tailorbird song. **DISTRIBUTION** Disjunct: Western and Eastern Ghats, foothills from SE Nepal eastwards, E Himalayas and much of north-east states. **HABITAT & HABITS** Occurs in forests, secondary growth, *nullahs* and *sholas*. Usually solitary; sometimes 2–3 birds in vicinity. Active, moving often between bush and canopy. Wild banana blossoms a favourite, the bird clinging upside down on bracts. Long, curved bill specially adapted to nectar diet.

Streaked Spiderhunter

House Sparrow ■ *Passer domesticus* 15cm

DESCRIPTION Male: grey crown and rump; chestnut neck-sides and nape; black streaks on chestnut-rufous back; black chin, centre of throat and breast; white ear-coverts. The **Spanish Sparrow** *P. hispaniolensis* male has chestnut crown and black streaks on flanks. Female: dull grey-brown above, streaked darker; dull whitish-brown below. **FOOD** Seeds; also insects, and often omnivorous. **VOICE** Noisy; medley of chirping notes; breeding male utters richer notes. **DISTRIBUTION** Subcontinent, to about 4,000m in Himalayas. **HABITAT & HABITS** Occurs in human habitation and cultivation. Small parties to large gatherings. Mostly commensal on man, feeding and nesting in and around human habitation, including most crowded localities. Hundreds roost together.

ABOVE: *Spanish Sparrow*

Russet Sparrow ■ *Passer cinnamomeus* 15cm

DESCRIPTION Male: rufous-chestnut above, streaked black on back; whitish wing-bars; black chin and centre of throat, bordered with dull yellow. Female: brown above, streaked darker; pale supercilium and wings-bars; dull ashy-yellow below. The **Eurasian Tree Sparrow** *P. montanus* male has black patch on white ear-coverts and lacks yellow on throat-sides. **FOOD** Seeds and insects. **VOICE** Chirping notes, *swee…* Indian Robin-like call (p. 121). **DISTRIBUTION** Himalayas; north-east; breeds 1,200–2,600m, higher to about 4,000m in north-east; descends in winter. **HABITAT & HABITS** Occurs in cultivation, edges of forest and mountain habitation. Gregarious mountain bird. Mostly feeds on the ground, picking seeds. May associate with similar birds. Often perches on dry branches and overhead wires.

Eurasian Tree Sparrow

Tibetan Snowfinch
■ *Montifringilla adamsi* 17cm

DESCRIPTION Dull grey-brown above with some streaking on back (less pronounced in juvenile and fresh plumage); blackish wing with white panel in wing-coverts; male has greyish-black bib (not usually seen in female); breeding male has black bill; in flight shows obvious white wing-patch; white tail with central black feathers and narrow black terminal band. Gregarious and often seen in flocks or around human habitation. **FOOD** Insects and seeds. **VOICE** Calls include hard *pink pink* and soft mewing. **DISTRIBUTION** Breeding resident in Himalayas at high altitudes above 3,600m (lower in winter). **HABITAT** High-altitude scrub, meadows, rocky bushy slopes and hillsides.

Streaked Weaver ■ *Ploceus manyar* 15cm

DESCRIPTION Breeding male: yellow crown; blackish head-sides; fulvous streaks on dark brown back; heavily streaked lower throat and breast. Female and non-breeding male: streaked above; yellow stripe over eye continues to behind ear-coverts; very pale below, boldly streaked on throat and breast. Eastern race *peguensis* darker and much more rufous above. The **Black-breasted Weaver** *P. benghalensis* male has dark breast-band. **FOOD** Seeds, grains and insects. **VOICE**

High-pitched chirping, wheezy notes and chatter, much like the Baya Weaver's (below). **DISTRIBUTION** Most of India south of Himalayas; absent in parts of Rajasthan and north-west regions. **HABITAT & HABITS** Occurs in reed beds, tall grass in well-watered areas and marshes. Gregarious. Active, as a rule not flying into trees; often nests close to other weavers.

ABOVE: *Black-breasted Weaver*

Baya Weaver ■ *Ploceus philippinus* 15cm

DESCRIPTION Breeding male: bright yellow crown; dark brown above, streaked yellow; dark brown ear-coverts and throat; yellow breast. Female: buffy-yellow above, streaked darker; pale supercilium and throat, turning buffy-yellow on breast, streaked on sides. Non-breeding male: bolder streaking than female; yellow restricted to crown in male of eastern race *burmanicus*. **FOOD** Grains, seeds, insects and nectar. **VOICE** Breeding

male has chirping and high-pitched, wheezy notes; very noisy at nest colony (monsoons). **DISTRIBUTION** Most of India to about 1,000m in outer Himalayas; absent in Kashmir. **HABITAT & HABITS** Inhabits open country, and tree- and palm-dotted cultivation. Gregarious. One of the most familiar and common birds of India, best known for its nest. Keeps to cultivated areas interspersed with trees. Feeds on the ground and in standing crops.

Red Avadavat
▪ *Amandava amandava* 10cm

DESCRIPTION Breeding male: crimson and brown, spotted white on wings and flanks; white-tipped tail. Female: brown above, spotted on wings; crimson rump; dull white throat; buffy-grey breast, yellow-brown below. Non-breeding male: like female, but greyer throat; upper breast distinctive. **FOOD** Grass seeds; also insects when breeding. **VOICE** Shrill, high-pitched notes, also uttered in flight. **DISTRIBUTION** Subcontinent, south of Himalayan foothills. **HABITAT & HABITS** Found in tall grass, reeds, sugar cane, scrub and gardens. Occurs in small flocks, often with other weavers. Partial to tall grass and scrub, preferably around well-watered areas. Active, vibrant and rather confiding. Huge numbers captured for bird markets.

Indian Silverbill
▪ *Euodice malabarica* 10cm

DESCRIPTION Sexes alike. Dull-brown above, with white rump; very dark, almost black wings; pointed tail; pale buffy-white below, with some brown on flanks; thick, grey-blue or slaty bill striking. **FOOD** Small seeds, millet. **VOICE** Faint *tee...tee...* notes; sometimes also whistling note. **DISTRIBUTION** Subcontinent to about 1,500m in Himalayas, chiefly outer ranges. **HABITAT & HABITS** Prefers dry areas; cultivation, scrub, grass and sometimes light, open forests. Gregarious. Mostly keeps to scrub in open country. Feeds on the ground and on standing crops, especially millet. Overall a rather 'dull' bird, in colour and demeanour.

Scaly-breasted Munia ▪ *Lonchura punctulata* 10cm

DESCRIPTION Sexes alike. Chocolate-brown above; olivish-yellow, pointed tail; white bars on rump; chestnut face-sides, chin and throat; white below, thickly speckled with very dark brown on breast, flanks and part of belly (speckles may be absent in winter and much of summer). **FOOD** Seeds and small berries; also insects. **VOICE** Common call a double-noted *ki…tee…ki…tee*. **DISTRIBUTION** Most of India, to about 1,500m in parts of Himalayas; absent in much of Punjab, north-west regions and W Rajasthan. **HABITAT & HABITS** Favours open scrub and cultivation, especially where interspersed with trees; also gardens. Sociable, moving in flocks of six to several dozen birds, often with other munias and weaver birds. Feeds on the ground and in low bushes, but rests in trees.

Black-headed Munia ▪ *Lonchura malacca* 10cm

DESCRIPTION Sexes alike. Black head, throat, breast, belly-centre and thighs; rufous-chestnut back, deeper chestnut on rump; white upper belly and sides of underbody. White

of lower parts replaced by chestnut in the **Chestnut Munia** *L. atricapilla* of north-east India. **FOOD** Grass seeds and paddy; occasionally insects. **VOICE** Faint *pee…pee…* calls. **DISTRIBUTION** Foothills and terai from SE Punjab eastwards; most of north-east, Orissa; peninsular India south of line from Mumbai to S

Madhya Pradesh. **HABITAT & HABITS** Inhabits reed beds, paddy, grass and scrub. Gregarious, except when breeding, as in other munias. Prefers reed beds and cultivation, especially where flooded. During breeding season (rains), often seen with the Streaked Weaver

ABOVE: *Chestnut Munia*   (p. 140); feeds on the ground.

Robin Accentor ■ *Prunella rubeculoides* 17cm

DESCRIPTION Sexes alike. Pale brown above, streaked darker on back; grey head and throat; two whitish wing-bars; rufous breast and creamy-white belly; streaks on flanks. **FOOD** Insects and small seeds. **VOICE** Sharp, trilling note; also *tszi...tszi...*; short, chirping song. **DISTRIBUTION** High Himalayas; breeds 3,200–5,300m; descends in winter to about 2,000m, rarely below 1,500m. **HABITAT & HABITS** Inhabits damp grass and scrub; high-altitude human habitation. Flocks in winter occasionally with other accentors, pipits and sparrows. Rather tame and confiding around high-altitude human habitation. Hops on the ground. Flies into bushes if intruded on beyond a point.

Rufous-breasted Accentor

■ *Prunella strophiata* 17cm

DESCRIPTION Sexes alike. Small chestnut and brown accentor; heavily streaked throat; brown-streaked crown and upperparts; orange supercilium with white in front of eyes and buffy-white moustache. **FOOD** Insects and small seeds. **VOICE** Sharp, trilling note; also *twitt...twitt...*; short, chirping song. **DISTRIBUTION** Himalayas: breeds at 2,700–5,000m; descends to about 1,200m in summer, rarely below 600m. **HABITAT & HABITS** Occurs in montane scrub and high-altitude human habitation. Descends lower in winter to bushy and fallow fields. Nests in low bushes on hillsides.

Citrine Wagtail ■ *Motacilla citreola* 17cm

DESCRIPTION Grey back; diagnostic yellow head, sides of face and complete underbody; white in dark wings. Race *calcarata* has deep-black back and rump; yellow of head may be paler in female; plumage of races often confusing. **FOOD** Insects and small snails. **VOICE** Ordinary call note a wheezy *tzzeep*, quite similar to that of the **Yellow Wagtail** M. *flava*. **DISTRIBUTION** Winter visitor to most of India; race *calcarata* breeds in Ladakh, Lahaul and Spiti, and Kashmir, at 1,500–4,600m. **HABITAT** Occurs in marshes, wet cultivation and jheel edges. Sociable, often with other wagtails. Shows marked preference for damp areas. Sometimes moves on floating vegetation on pond surfaces. Either walks cautiously or makes short dashes.

ABOVE: *Yellow Wagtail*

Grey Wagtail ■ *Motacilla cinerea* 17cm

DESCRIPTION Breeding male: grey above; white supercilium; brownish wings with yellow-white band; yellow-green at tail-base (rump); blackish tail with white outer feathers; black throat and white malar stripe; yellow below. Wintering male and female: whitish throat (sometimes mottled black in breeding female); paler yellow below. **FOOD** Insects and small molluscs. **VOICE** Sharp *tzitsi…* calls, uttered on the wing; breeding male has pleasant song and display flight. **DISTRIBUTION** Breeds in Himalayas, from Baluchistan east to Nepal, 1,200–4,300m; winters from foothills south throughout India. **HABITAT & HABITS** Inhabits rocky mountain streams in summer; open areas, forest clearings and watersides in winter. Mostly solitary or in pairs. Typical wagtail, feeding on the ground, incessantly wagging tail. Settles on house roofs and overhead wires.

White-browed Wagtail
■ *Motacilla maderaspatensis* 21cm

DESCRIPTION Black above; prominent white supercilium and large wing-band; black throat and breast; white below. Female usually browner where male is black. Black-backed races of the **White Wagtail** M. *alba* have conspicuous white foreheads. **FOOD** Insects. **VOICE** Sharp *tzizit* or *cheezit…* call; breeding male has pleasant whistling song. **DISTRIBUTION** Most of India south of Himalayan foothills to about 1,200m; only resident wagtail in Indian plains, breeding to 2,000m in peninsula mountains. **HABITAT & HABITS** Found around rocky streams, rivers, ponds and tanks; may sometimes enter wet cultivation. Mostly in pairs, though small parties may feed together in winter. Bird of flowing waters, especially rock-strewn rivers, though may be seen on ponds and tanks. Feeds at edge of water, wagging tail frequently. Also rides on ferry boats plying rivers.

White Wagtail

Paddyfield Pipit ■ *Anthus rufulus* 15cm

DESCRIPTION Sexes alike. Fulvous-brown above, with dark brown feather-centres, giving distinctive appearance; dark brown tail, with white outer feathers, easily seen in flight; dull-fulvous below, streaked dark brown on sides of throat, neck and entire breast. Winter-visiting **Tawny Pipit** A. *campestris* usually lacks streaks on underbody, while **Blyth's Pipit** A. *godlewskii* is indistinguishable in the field, except by its harsher call note. **FOOD** Insects, seeds and spiders. **VOICE** Thin *tsip, tseep* and *tsip…tseep…* calls; breeding male has trilling song. **DISTRIBUTION** To about 2,000m in outer Himalayas, south throughout India. **HABITAT & HABITS** Occupies grassland, marshy ground and cultivation. Occurs in pairs or several scattered on the ground. Runs in short spurts. When disturbed, utters feeble note as it takes off. Singing males perch on grass tufts and small bushes.

ABOVE: *Tawny Pipit*

Blyth's Pipit

Olive-backed Pipit ■ *Anthus hodgsoni* 15cm

DESCRIPTION Sexes alike. Olive-brown above, streaked dark brown; dull-white supercilium, two wing-bars and in outer-tail feathers; pale buff-white below, profusely

streaked dark brown on entire breast and flanks. The **Tree Pipit** *A. trivialis* brown above, without olive wash. **FOOD** Insects, and grass and other seeds. **VOICE** Faint *tseep...* call; breeding male has lark-like song. **DISTRIBUTION** Breeds in Himalayas, east from W Himachal Pradesh; above 2,700m to timberline; winters in foothills and almost all over India, except arid north-west, Kutch; *trivialis* breeds only in NW Himalayas and is most common in winter over C India,

ABOVE: *Tree Pipit*

but sporadically over range of *hodgsoni*. **HABITAT & HABITS** Inhabits forests and grassy slopes. Gregarious in winter; spends most time on the ground, running briskly. If approached close, flies with *tseep...* call into trees; descends in a few minutes.

Red-fronted Serin ■ *Serinus pusillus* 13cm

DESCRIPTION Sexes alike. Scarlet-orange forehead; blackish-grey crown; buffy back, streaked dark; yellow-orange rump and shoulder; yellow wing-edges and whitish wing-

bars; sooty-brown below, with grey and buff; dull yellow-buff belly and flanks, streaked brown. **FOOD** Flower and grass seeds; small berries. **VOICE** Pleasant twittering *chrr...chrr*; faint *tree... tree...* call note. **DISTRIBUTION** W Himalayas, extreme west to Uttarakhand; 750–4,500m; breeds mostly at 2,400–4,000m. **HABITAT & HABITS** Occurs in rocky, bush-covered mountainsides. Gregarious. Quite active and constantly on the move. Feeds on flower-heads and on the ground. Drinks and bathes often. Spends considerable time in bushes and low trees.

Eastern Goldfinch ■ *Carduelis caniceps* 14cm

DESCRIPTION Sexes alike. Crimson forehead; greyish-brown above, with large white rump-patch; black and yellow wings striking, at rest and in flight. Young birds have streaked upperparts. **FOOD** Seeds of flowers, especially thistle and sunflowers. **VOICE** Ordinary call note a somewhat liquid *witwit…witwit…*; pleasant, twittering song; also *chhrrik* call. **DISTRIBUTION** Himalayas, extreme west to around C Nepal; breeds mostly at 2,000–4,000m, ascending somewhat more; descends into foothills in winter. **HABITAT & HABITS** Occurs in open coniferous forests, orchards, cultivation and scrub. Sociable; flock size ranges from four to several dozen birds, sometimes with other finches. Forages on the ground; also attends to flower-heads. Undulating, somewhat dancing flight.

Plain Mountain Finch ■ *Leucosticte nemoricola* 15cm

DESCRIPTION Sexes alike. Grey-brown above, streaked dark brown; greyer on rump; pale buffy bar and markings in dark brown wings; dull grey-brown below, streaked browner on breast-sides and flanks. **Brandt's Mountain Finch** *L. brandti* (18cm) darker above, with rosy-pink rump and white in outer tail. Finches with plenty of white in their wings, generally found in high Tibetan country of Himalayas, are usually snowfinches. **FOOD** Grass and other seeds; small insects. **VOICE** Twittering and chattering notes, rather sparrow-like in tone; calls often. **DISTRIBUTION** High Himalayas, breeding at 3,200–4,800m (above timberline); descends in winter, occasionally to as low as 1,000m. **HABITAT & HABITS** Occurs in open meadows, dwarf scrub and cultivation. Gregarious. Good-sized flocks on the ground, among stones. Sometimes with other finches and buntings. Calls often when feeding.

Brandt's Mountain Finch

Common Rosefinch ■ *Carpodacus erythrinus* 15cm

DESCRIPTION Male: crimson above, tinged brown; dark eye-stripe; crimson rump and underbody, fading to dull rose-white belly. Female: buff-brown above, streaked dark; two pale wing-bars; dull buff below, streaked, except on belly. Male **Pink-browed Rosefinch** *C. rodochroa* has pink supercilium, rump and underparts. **FOOD** Crop seeds, fruits, buds and nectar. **VOICE** Rather quiet in winter; pleasant song of to eight notes; may sing before departure from wintering grounds; also double-noted, questioning *twee…ee* call. **DISTRIBUTION** Breeds in Himalayas, 2,700–4,000m; winters over most of India. **HABITAT & HABITS** Found in cultivation, open forests, gardens and bushes. Occurs in small flocks. Feeds on bushes and crops. Often descends to the ground. Associates with other birds.

Pink-browed Rosefinch

White-browed Rosefinch ■ *Carpodacus thura* 17cm

DESCRIPTION Male: brown above, streaked blackish; pink and white forehead and supercilium; dark eye-stripe; rose-pink rump and double wing-bar. Female: streaked brown; broad, whitish supercilium and single wing-bar; yellow rump; buffy below, streaked. White in supercilium easily identifies this species. **FOOD** Seeds and berries. **VOICE** Calls often when feeding on the ground; fairly loud *pupuepipi…* call. **DISTRIBUTION** Himalayas, breeding at 3,000–4,000m; winters to about 1,800m. **HABITAT & HABITS** Found in treeline forests, fir, juniper and rhododendron; open mountainsides and bushes in winter. Occurs in small flocks, sometimes with other finches. Mostly feeds on the ground, but settles on bushes and small trees.

Red-headed Bullfinch ■ *Pyrrhula erythrocephala* 17cm

DESCRIPTION Male: black around base of bill and eye; brick-red crown; grey back; white rump; glossy purple-black wings; forked tail; black chin; rust-red below; ashy-white belly. Female: like male, but olive-yellow on crown; grey-brown back and underbody. **FOOD** Seeds, buds and berries; also flower nectar. **VOICE** Single or double-noted *pheu... pheu...* call. **DISTRIBUTION** Himalayas, Kashmir to extreme east; breeds at 2,400–4,000m; descends in winter to about 1,200m. **HABITAT & HABITS** Found in forests and bushes, in small parties, occasionally with other birds. Feeds in low bushes, sometimes on the ground. Bird of cover, rather quiet and secretive.

Black-and-yellow Grosbeak ■ *Mycerobas icterioides* 22cm

DESCRIPTION Male: black head, throat, wings, tail and thighs; yellow collar, back and underbody below breast; thick, finch-like bill. Female: grey above; buffy rump and belly. Very similar male **Collared Grosbeak** M. *affinis* brighter yellow (often with orangish wash), with yellow thighs. **FOOD** Conifer seeds and shoots; also berries and insects. **VOICE** Loud 2–3-noted whistle is familiar bird call of W Himalayas; loud *chuck...chuck* note when feeding; male has rich song. **DISTRIBUTION** W Himalayas to C Nepal. **HABITAT & HABITS** Inhabits mountain forests. Occurs in small parties in tall coniferous forest. Feeds on the ground and on bushes, but spends much time in higher branches, where difficult to see. Rather noisy.

Collared Grosbeak

Rock Bunting ■ *Emberiza cia* 15cm

DESCRIPTION Male: blue-grey head with black coronal stripe, eye-stripe and malar stripe, the latter curled and meeting eye-stripe diagnostic; whitish supercilium and cheeks; pale chestnut-brown back, streaked dark; unmarked rump; white outer sides of dark tail

distinctive; blue-grey throat and breast; rufous-chestnut below. Female: slightly duller. Male **Chestnut-eared Bunting** *E. fucata* has black-streaked grey head, white throat and breast, and chestnut ear-coverts. **FOOD** Seeds and small insects. **VOICE** Squeaky *tsip…tsip…* note; calls often; common bird call of W Himalayas; squeaky song of several notes. **DISTRIBUTION** All of Himalayas at 1,500–4,200m; most common in W Himalayas; winters in foothills and plains of India, coming as far south as Delhi. **HABITAT & HABITS**

Occurs in grassy, rocky hillsides in open forests; cultivation and scrub. Solitary or in small parties. Active and restless. Mostly feeds on the ground; meadows, paths and roads. Flicks tail often. Regularly settles on bushes and trees.

RIGHT: *Chestnut-eared Bunting*

Grey-necked Bunting

■ *Emberiza buchanani* 15cm

DESCRIPTION Male: grey head with white eye-ring; brown back with faint rufous wash and dark streaks; white edges to dark tail; whitish throat, mottled rufous; dark moustachial stripe, not easily visible; pale rufous-chestnut below. Female: somewhat duller; more prominent moustachial stripe. **FOOD** Grass seeds; sometimes grains. **VOICE** Faint single note. **DISTRIBUTION** Winter visitor; quite common over W and C India-Gujarat, S and W Rajasthan, SW Uttar Pradesh, south through W and C Madhya Pradesh, Maharashtra and parts of Karnataka. **HABITAT & HABITS** Found in open, rocky, grassy country and scrub. Occurs in small flocks. Feeds mostly on the ground, sometimes with other birds. Quite active.

White-capped Bunting ■ *Emberiza stewarti* 15cm

DESCRIPTION Male: grey-white top of head; black eye-stripe, whitish cheeks, and black chin and upper throat distinctive; chestnut back and rump; white outer tail; white breast with chestnut gorget below; dull fulvous below; chestnut flanks. Female: lacks black and white head pattern of male; brown above, streaked; rufous-chestnut rump; fulvous-buff below, with rufous breast. **FOOD** Mainly grass seeds. **VOICE** Faint but sharp *tsit…* or *chit…* note. **DISTRIBUTION** Breeds in W Himalayas, extreme west to Uttarakhand, 1,500–3,500m; winters in W Himalayan foothills, and over extensive parts of W and C India, south to Maharashtra. **HABITAT & HABITS** Found in open, grass-covered, rocky hillsides and scrub. Occurs in small flocks, often with other buntings and finches. Feeds on the ground. Rests in bushes and trees.

Crested Bunting ■ *Melophus lathami* 15cm

DESCRIPTION Male: striking glossy black plumage, with long, pointed crest and chestnut wings and tail. Female: crested; olive-brown above, streaked darker; rufous in wings distinctive; buffy-yellow below, streaked dark on breast; darkish moustachial stripe. **FOOD** Grass seeds; presumably also insects. **VOICE** Faint *chip…* call; breeding male has pleasant, though somewhat monotonous, song (May–August). **DISTRIBUTION** Resident over wide part of India, from outer Himalayas to about 1,800m; south to SW Maharashtra and Andhra Pradesh; appears to move considerably after rains. **HABITAT & HABITS** Found in open bush, rock-covered mountainsides, and open country; sometimes also cultivation. Occurs in small flocks, often spread wide over an area. Feeds on the ground, on paths, meadows and tar roads, especially along mountainsides. Perches on ruins, walls, stones and low bushes. On the ground, an active and upright bird.

| # | Protected by NPWC Act 1973 (2029 BS) |

CR Critically Endangered

EN Endangered

VU Vulnerable

Bold italic (**CR, EN, VU**) indicate globally threatened

Regular (CR, EN, VU) indicate nationally threatened

Common English Name	Scientific Name	Status
GALLIFORMES		
Phasianidae (Partridges & Pheasants)		
Snow Partridge	*Lerwa lerwa*	
Hill Partridge	*Arborophila torqueola*	
Rufous-throated Partridge	*Arborophila rufogularis*	
Tibetan Partridge	*Perdix hodgsoniae*	
Common Quail	*Coturnix coturnix*	
Rain Quail	*Coturnix coromandelica*	
Asian Blue Quail	*Synoicus chinensis*	CR
Jungle Bush-quail	*Perdicula asiatica*	
Himalayan Snowcock	*Tetraogallus himalayensis*	
Tibetan Snowcock	*Tetraogallus tibetanus*	I
Chukar	*Alectoris chukar*	
Black Francolin	*Francolinus francolinus*	
Grey Francolin	*Francolinus pondicerianus*	VU
Swamp Francolin	*Francolinus gularis*	**VU**, EN
Indian Peafowl	*Pavo cristatus*	III
Red Junglefowl	*Gallus gallus*	
Himalayan Monal	*Lophophorus impejanus*	I, #
Satyr Tragopan	*Tragopan satyra*	III, #, VU
Blood Pheasant	*Ithaginis cruentus*	II
Koklass Pheasant	*Pucrasia macrolopha*	III, VU
Cheer Pheasant	*Catreus wallichii*	**VU**, I, #, EN
Kalij Pheasant	*Lophura leucomelanos*	III
ANSERIFORMES		
Anatidae (Ducks, Geese & Swans)		
Fulvous Whistling-duck	*Dendrocygna bicolor*	III
Lesser Whistling-duck	*Dendrocygna javanica*	
Whooper Swan	*Cygnus cygnus*	
Tundra Swan	*Cygnus columbianus*	
Bean Goose	*Anser fabalis*	
Bar-headed Goose	*Anser indicus*	
Greater White-fronted Goose	*Anser albifrons*	
Greylag Goose	*Anser anser*	
Long-tailed Duck	*Clangula hyemalis*	**VU**
Common Goldeneye	*Bucephala clangula*	

Common English Name	Scientific Name	Status
Smew	*Mergellus albellus*	
Goosander	*Mergus merganser*	
Red-breasted Merganser	*Mergus serrator*	
Ruddy Shelduck	*Tadorna ferruginea*	
Common Shelduck	*Tadorna tadorna*	
African Comb Duck	*Sarkidiornis melanotos*	II, EN
Cotton Pygmy-goose	*Nettapus coromandelianus*	VU
Red-crested Pochard	*Netta rufina*	
Common Pochard	*Aythya ferina*	**VU**
Baer's Pochard	*Aythya baeri*	**CR**, CR
Ferruginous Duck	*Aythya nyroca*	VU
Tufted Duck	*Aythya fuligula*	
Greater Scaup	*Aythya marila*	
Pink-headed Duck	*Rhodonessa caryophyllacea*	CR, I
Garganey	*Spatula querquedula*	VU
Northern Shoveler	*Spatula clypeata*	
Falcated Duck	*Mareca falcata*	CR
Mandarin Duck	*Aix galericulata*	
Gadwall	*Mareca strepera*	
Eurasian Wigeon	*Mareca penelope*	
Indian Spot-billed Duck	*Anas poecilorhyncha*	
Chinese Spot-billed Duck	*Anas zonorhyncha*	
Mallard	*Anas platyrhynchos*	
Northern Pintail	*Anas acuta*	EN
Common Teal	*Anas crecca*	
Baikal Teal	*Sibirionetta formosa*	II
PODICIPEDIFORMES		
Podicipedidae (Grebes)		
Little Grebe	*Tachybaptus ruficollis*	
Great Crested Grebe	*Podiceps cristatus*	
Black-necked Grebe	*Podiceps nigricollis*	
PHOENICOPTERIFORMES		
Phoenicopteridae (Flamingos)		
Greater Flamingo	*Phoenicopterus roseus*	
COLUMBIFORMES		
Columbidae (Pigeons & Doves)		
Rock Dove	*Columba livia*	
Hill Pigeon	*Columba rupestris*	
Snow Pigeon	*Columba leuconota*	
Common Woodpigeon	*Columba palumbus*	
Speckled Wood Pigeon	*Columba hodgsonii*	
Ashy Wood Pigeon	*Columba pulchricollis*	
Oriental Turtle-dove	*Streptopelia orientalis*	
Eurasian Collared Dove	*Streptopelia decaocto*	
Red Collared Dove	*Streptopelia tranquebarica*	
Spotted Dove	*Stigmatopelia chinensis*	
Laughing Dove	*Stigmatopelia senegalensis*	
Barred Cuckoo-dove	*Macropygia unchall*	VU
Emerald Dove	*Chalcophaps indica*	
Orange-breasted Green-pigeon	*Treron bicinctus*	
Ashy-headed Green-pigeon	*Treron phayrei*	

Common English Name	Scientific Name	Status
Thick-billed Green-pigeon	*Treron curvirostra*	EN
Yellow-footed Green Pigeon	*Treron phoenicopterus*	
Pin-tailed Green Pigeon	*Treron apicauda*	
Wedge-tailed Green Pigeon	*Treron sphenurus*	
Mountain Imperial-pigeon	*Ducula badia*	CR
PTEROCLIFORMES		
Pteroclidae (Sandgrouse)		
Tibetan Sandgrouse	*Syrrhaptes tibetanus*	VU
CAPRIMULGIFORMES		
Caprimulgidae (Nightjars)		
Grey Nightjar	*Caprimulgus jotaka*	
Sykes's Nightjar	*Caprimulgus mahrattensis*	
Large-tailed Nightjar	*Caprimulgus macrurus*	
Indian Nightjar	*Caprimulgus asiaticus*	EN
Savanna Nightjar	*Caprimulgus affinis*	
Hemiprocnidae (Treeswifts)		
Crested Treeswift	*Hemiprocne coronata*	
Apodidae (Swifts)		
White-rumped Spinetail	*Zoonavena sylvatica*	
White-throated Needletail	*Hirundapus caudacutus*	
Silver-backed Needletail	*Hirundapus cochinchinensis*	
Himalayan Swiftlet	*Aerodramus brevirostris*	
Asian Palm-swift	*Cypsiurus balasiensis*	
Alpine Swift	*Tachymarptis melba*	
Pacific Swift	*Apus pacificus*	
House Swift	*Apus nipalensis*	
Common Swift	*Apus apus*	
CUCULIFORMES		
Cuculidae (Cuckoos)		
Greater Coucal	*Centropus sinensis*	
Lesser Coucal	*Centropus bengalensis*	
Sirkeer Malkoha	*Taccocua leschenaultii*	
Green-billed Malkoha	*Phaenicophaeus tristis*	
Jacobin Cuckoo	*Clamator jacobinus*	
Chestnut-winged Cuckoo	*Clamator coromandus*	
Asain Koel	*Eudynamys scolopaceus*	
Asian Emerald Cuckoo	*Chrysococcyx maculatus*	
Banded Bay Cuckoo	*Cacomantis sonneratii*	
Grey-bellied Cuckoo	*Cacomantis passerinus*	
Fork-tailed Drongo Cuckoo	*Surniculus dicruroides*	
Large Hawk Cuckoo	*Hierococcyx sparverioides*	
Common Hawk Cuckoo	*Hierococcyx varius*	
Whistling Hawk Cuckoo	*Hierococcyx nisicolor*	
Indian Cuckoo	*Cuculus micropterus*	
Common Cuckoo	*Cuculus canorus*	
Eurasian Cuckoo	*Cuculus canorus*	
Lesser Cuckoo	*Cuculus poliocephalus*	
Oriental Cuckoo	*Cuculus saturatus*	
Plaintive Cuckoo	*Cacomantis merulinus*	
GRUIFORMES		
Rallidae (Rails)		
Slaty-breasted Rail	*Lewinia striata*	

Common English Name	Scientific Name	Status
Eastern Water Rail	*Rallus indicus*	
Western Water Rail	*Rallus aquaticus*	CR
Ruddy-breasted Crake	*Zapornia fusca*	
Brown Crake	*Zapornia akool*	
Baillon's Crake	*Zapornia pusilla*	VU
Black-tailed Crake	*Zapornia bicolor*	
Spotted Crake	*Porzana porzana*	
Slaty-legged Crake	*Rallina eurizonoides*	EN
White-breasted Waterhen	*Amaurornis phoenicurus*	
Watercock	*Gallicrex cinerea*	
Purple Swamphen	*Porphyrio porphyrio*	
Common Moorhen	*Gallinula chloropus*	
Common Coot	*Fulica atra*	
Gruidae (Cranes)		
Sarus Crane	*Antigone antigone*	**VU**, II, ≠, VU
Demoiselle Crane	*Grus virgo*	II, VU
Common Crane	*Grus grus*	II
Black-necked Crane	*Grus nigricollis*	**VU**, I
GAVIIFORMES		
Gaviidae (Loons)		
Red-throated Loon	*Gavia stellata*	
OTIDIFORMES		
Otididae (Bustards)		
Bengal Florican	*Houbaropsis bengalensis*	**CR**, I, ≠, CR
Lesser Florican	*Sypheotides indicus*	**EN**, II, ≠, CR
Ciconiidae (Storks)		
Greater Adjutant	*Leptoptilos dubius*	**EN**, CR
Lesser Adjutant	*Leptoptilos javanicus*	**VU**, VU
Painted Stork	*Mycteria leucocephala*	EN
Asian Openbill	*Anastomus oscitans*	VU
Black Stork	*Ciconia nigra*	II, ≠, VU
Asian Woollyneck	*Ciconia episcopus*	**VU**
White Stork	*Ciconia ciconia*	≠
Black-necked Stork	*Ephippiorhynchus asiaticus*	CR
Threskiornithidae (Ibises & Spoonbills)		
Eurasian Spoonbill	*Platalea leucorodia*	II, CR
Black-headed Ibis	*Threskiornis melanocephalus*	
Red-naped Ibis	*Pseudibis papillosa*	
Glossy Ibis	*Plegadis falcinellus*	
PELECANIFORMES		
Ardeidae (Herons, Egrets & Bitterns)		
Eurasian Bittern	*Botaurus stellaris*	EN
Yellow Bittern	*Ixobrychus sinensis*	
Cinnamon Bittern	*Ixobrychus cinnamomeus*	
Black Bittern	*Ixobrychus flavicollis*	EN
Malay Night-heron	*Gorsachius melanolophus*	CR
Black-crowned Night-heron	*Nycticorax nycticorax*	
Green-backed Heron	*Butorides striata*	
Indian Pond-heron	*Ardeola grayii*	
Cattle Egret	*Bubulcus ibis*	
Grey Heron	*Ardea cinerea*	
White-bellied Heron	*Ardea insignis*	**CR**

Common English Name	Scientific Name	Status
Purple Heron	*Ardea purpurea*	
Great White Egret	*Ardea alba*	
Intermediate Egret	*Ardea intermedia*	
Little Egret	*Egretta garzetta*	
Pelecanidae (Pelicans)		
Spot-billed Pelican	*Pelecanus philippensis*	CR
Great White Pelican	*Pelecanus onocrotalus*	
SULIFORMES		
Phalacrocoracidae (Cormorants & Shags)		
Little Cormorant	*Microcarbo niger*	
Great Cormorant	*Phalacrocorax carbo*	
Indian Cormorant	*Phalacrocorax fuscicollis*	
Anhingidae (Darters)		
Oriental Darter	*Anhinga melanogaster*	
CHARADRIIFORMES		
Burhinidae (Thick-knees)		
Indian Thick-knee	*Burhinus indicus*	
Great Thick-knee	*Esacus recurvirostris*	CR
Haematopodidae (Oystercatchers)		
Eurasian Oystercatcher	*Haematopus ostralegus*	
Ibidorhynchidae (Ibisbill)		
Ibisbill	*Ibidorhyncha struthersii*	EN
Recurvirostridae (Avocets & Stilts)		
Pied Avocet	*Recurvirostra avosetta*	
Black-winged Stilt	*Himantopus himantopus*	
Charadriidae (Plovers, Dotterels & Lapwings)		
Grey Plover	*Pluvialis squatarola*	
Pacific Golden Plover	*Pluvialis fulva*	
Long-billed Plover	*Charadrius placidus*	
Little Ringed Plover	*Charadrius dubius*	
Kentish Plover	*Charadrius alexandrinus*	
Lesser Sandplover	*Charadrius mongolus*	
Greater Sandplover	*Charadrius leschenaultii*	
Northern Lapwing	*Vanellus vanellus*	
River Lapwing	*Vanellus duvaucelii*	
Yellow-wattled Lapwing	*Vanellus malabaricus*	VU
Grey-headed Lapwing	*Vanellus cinereus*	
Red-wattled Lapwing	*Vanellus indicus*	
White-tailed Lapwing	*Vanellus leucurus*	
Rostratulidae (Painted-snipe)		
Greater Painted-snipe	*Rostratula benghalensis*	
Jacanidae (Jacanas)		
Pheasant-tailed Jacana	*Hydrophasianus chirurgus*	VU
Bronze-winged Jacana	*Metopidius indicus*	
Scolopacidae (Sandpipers)		
Red Knot	*Calidris canutus*	
Terek Sandpiper	*Xenus cinereus*	
Red-necked Phalarope	*Phalaropus lobatus*	
Whimbrel	*Numenius phaeopus*	
Eurasian Curlew	*Numenius arquata*	CR
Black-tailed Godwit	*Limosa limosa*	
Ruddy Turnstone	*Arenaria interpres*	

Common English Name	Scientific Name	Status
Ruff	*Calidris pugnax*	
Curlew Sandpiper	*Calidris ferruginea*	
Temminck's Stint	*Calidris temminckii*	
Long-toed Stint	*Calidris subminuta*	
Sanderling	*Calidris alba*	
Dunlin	*Calidris alpina*	
Little Stint	*Calidris minuta*	
Eurasian Woodcock	*Scolopax rusticola*	
Solitary Snipe	*Gallinago solitaria*	
Wood Snipe	*Gallinago nemoricola*	**VU**, VU
Pintail Snipe	*Gallinago stenura*	
Common Snipe	*Gallinago gallinago*	
Jack Snipe	*Lymnocryptes minimus*	
Common Sandpiper	*Actitis hypoleucos*	
Green Sandpiper	*Tringa ochropus*	
Spotted Redshank	*Tringa erythropus*	
Common Greenshank	*Tringa nebularia*	
Common Redshank	*Tringa totanus*	
Wood Sandpiper	*Tringa glareola*	
Marsh Sandpiper	*Tringa stagnatilis*	
Turnicidae (Buttonquail)		
Common Buttonquail	*Turnix sylvaticus*	
Yellow-legged Buttonquail	*Turnix tanki*	
Barred Buttonquail	*Turnix suscitator*	
Glareolidae (Pratincoles & Coursers)		
Indian Courser	*Cursorius coromandelicus*	EN
Oriental Pratincole	*Glareola maldivarum*	
Little Pratincole	*Glareola lactea*	
Laridae (Gulls, Terns & Skimmers)		
Indian Skimmer	*Rynchops albicollis*	**VU**, CR
Brown-headed Gull	*Larus brunnicephalus*	VU
Black-headed Gull	*Larus ridibundus*	VU
Pallas's Gull	*Larus ichthyaetus*	
Mew Gull	*Larus canus*	
Slender-billed Gull	*Larus genei*	
Lesser Black-backed Gull	*Larus fuscus*	
Little Tern	*Sternula albifrons*	VU
Caspian Tern	*Hydroprogne caspia*	CR
Whiskered Tern	*Chlidonias hybrida*	
White-winged Tern	*Chlidonias leucopterus*	
River Tern	*Sterna aurantia*	CR
Common Tern	*Sterna hirundo*	
Black-bellied Tern	*Sterna acuticauda*	**EN**, CR
Gull-billed Tern	*Gelochelidon nilotica*	CR
Sooty Tern	*Onychoprion fuscatus*	
STRIGIFORMES		
Tytonidae (Barn Owls)		
Eastern Grass-owl	*Tyto longimembris*	II, CR
Common Barn-owl	*Tyto alba*	II, VU
Strigidae (True Owls)		
Brown Boobook	*Ninox scutulata*	II
Collared Owlet	*Glaucidium brodiei*	II

Common English Name	Scientific Name	Status
Asian Barred Owlet	*Glaucidium cuculoides*	II
Jungle Owlet	*Glaucidium radiatum*	II
Spotted Owlet	*Athene brama*	II
Little Owl	*Athene noctua*	II
Collared Scops Owl	*Otus lettia*	II
Indian Scops Owl	*Otus bakkamoena*	II
Mountain Scops Owl	*Otus spilocephalus*	II
Oriental Scops Owl	*Otus sunia*	II
Short-eared Owl	*Asio flammeus*	II, VU
Northern Long-eared Owl	*Asio otus*	II
Brown Wood Oowl	*Strix leptogrammica*	II, VU
Himalayan Owl	*Strix nivicolum*	
Mottled Wood Owl	*Strix ocellata*	II
Eurasian Eagle Owl	*Bubo bubo*	II
Rock Eagle Owl	*Bubo bengalensis*	VU
Spot-bellied Eagle Owl	*Bubo nipalensis*	II, EN
Dusky Eagle Owl	*Bubo coromandus*	II, CR
Brown Fish Owl	*Ketupa zeylonensis*	II, VU
Tawny Fish Owl	*Ketupa flavipes*	II, CR
ACCIPITRIFORMES		
Pandionidae (Osprey)		
Osprey	*Pandion haliaetus*	II
Accipitridae (Kites, Hawks & Eagles)		
Black-winged Kite	*Elanus caeruleus*	II
Oriental Honey-buzzard	*Pernis ptilorhynchus*	II
Jerdon's Baza	*Aviceda jerdoni*	II, CR
Black Baza	*Aviceda leuphotes*	II
Crested Serpent Eagle	*Spilornis cheela*	II
Short-toed Snake-eagle	*Circaetus gallicus*	II
Bearded Vulture	*Gypaetus barbatus*	II, VU
Egyptian Vulture	*Neophron percnopterus*	**EN**, II, VU
Red-headed Vulture	*Sarcogyps calvus*	**CR**, II, EN
Himalayan Griffon	*Gyps himalayensis*	II, VU
White-rumped Vulture	*Gyps bengalensis*	**CR**, II, CR
Slender-billed Vulture	*Gyps tenuirostris*	CR, II, CR
Indian Vulture	*Gyps indicus*	**CR**, II
Griffon Vulture	*Gyps fulvus*	II
Cinereous Vulture	*Aegypius monachus*	II, EN
Mountain Hawk Eagle	*Nisaetus nipalensis*	II
Changeable Hawk Eagle	*Nisaetus cirrhatus*	II
Rufous-bellied Eagle	*Lophotriorchis kienerii*	II, CR
Black Eagle	*Ictinaetus malaiensis*	II
Indian Spotted Eagle	*Clanga hastata*	**VU**, II, VU
Greater Spotted Eagle	*Clanga clanga*	**VU**, II, VU
Tawny Eagle	*Aquila rapax*	II
Steppe Eagle	*Aquila nipalensis*	**EN**, II, VU
Eastern Imperial Eagle	*Aquila heliaca*	**VU**, I, CR
Golden Eagle	*Aquila chrysaetos*	II, VU
Bonelli's Eagle	*Aquila fasciata*	II
Booted Eagle	*Hieraaetus pennatus*	II
Western Marsh Harrier	*Circus aeruginosus*	II, VU
Eastern Marsh Harrier	*Circus spilonotus*	II

Common English Name	Scientific Name	Status
Hen Harrier	*Circus cyaneus*	II, VU
Pallid Harrier	*Circus macrourus*	II, VU
Pied Harrier	*Circus melanoleucos*	II, VU
Montagu's Harrier	*Circus pygargus*	II, CR
Crested Goshawk	*Accipiter trivirgatus*	II
Shikra	*Accipiter badius*	II
Besra	*Accipiter virgatus*	II
Eurasian Sparrowhawk	*Accipiter nisus*	II
Northern Goshawk	*Accipiter gentilis*	II
Pallas's Fish-eagle	*Haliaeetus leucoryphus*	**EN**, CR
White-tailed Sea-eagle	*Haliaeetus albicilla*	I, CR
Lesser Fish-eagle	*Icthyophaga humilis*	II, CR
Grey-headed Fish-eagle	*Icthyophaga ichthyaetus*	II, CR
Brahminy Kite	*Haliastur indus*	II, CR
Black Kite	*Milvus migrans*	II
White-eyed Buzzard	*Butastur teesa*	II
Himalayan Buzzard	*Buteo refectus*	II
Long-legged Buzzard	*Buteo rufinus*	II
Upland Buzzard	*Buteo hemilasius*	II
TROGONIFORMES		
Trogonidae (Trogons)		
Red-headed Trogon	*Harpactes erythrocephalus*	EN
BUCEROTIFORMES		
Bucerotidae (Hornbills)		
Great Hornbill	*Buceros bicornis*	I, #, EN
Indian Grey Hornbill	*Ocyceros birostris*	
Oriental Pied Hornbill	*Anthracoceros albirostris*	II
Rufous-necked Hornbill	*Aceros nipalensis*	**VU**, I
Upupidae (Hoopoes)		
Common Hoopoe	*Upupa epops*	
CORACIIFORMES		
Meropidae (Bee-eaters)		
Blue-bearded Bee-eater	*Nyctyornis athertoni*	
Green Bee-eater	*Merops orientalis*	
Chestnut-headed Bee-eater	*Merops leschenaulti*	
Blue-tailed Bee-eater	*Merops philippinus*	
Coraciidae (Rollers)		
Indian Roller	*Coracias benghalensis*	
Indochinese Roller	*Coracias affinis*	
Oriental Dollarbird	*Eurystomus orientalis*	
Alcedinidae (Kingfishers)		
Blue-eared Kingfisher	*Alcedo meninting*	EN
Common Kingfisher	*Alcedo atthis*	
Crested Kingfisher	*Megaceryle lugubris*	
Pied Kingfisher	*Ceryle rudis*	
Stork-billed Kingfisher	*Pelargopsis capensis*	
Ruddy Kingfisher	*Halcyon coromanda*	CR
White-throated Kingfisher	*Halcyon smyrnensis*	
Blyth's Kingfisher	*Alcedo hercules*	CR
Black-capped Kingfisher	*Halcyon pileata*	
PICIFORMES		
Megalaimidae (Asian Barbets)		

Common English Name	Scientific Name	Status
Coppersmith Barbet	*Psilopogon haemacephalus*	
Blue-eared Barbet	*Psilopogon cyanotis*	CR
Great Barbet	*Psilopogon virens*	
Lineated Barbet	*Psilopogon lineatus*	
Brown-headed Barbet	*Psilopogon zeylanicus*	
Golden-throated Barbet	*Psilopogon franklinii*	
Blue-throated Barbet	*Psilopogon asiaticus*	
Indicatoridae (Honeyguides)		
Yellow-rumped Honeyguide	*Indicator xanthonotus*	EN
Picidae (Woodpeckers)		
Eurasian Wryneck	*Jynx torquilla*	
White-browed Piculet	*Sasia ochracea*	CR
Speckled Piculet	*Picumnus innominatus*	
Bay Woodpecker	*Blythipicus pyrrhotis*	
Greater Flameback	*Chrysocolaptes guttacristatus*	
White-naped Woodpecker	*Chrysocolaptes festivus*	
Himalayan Flameback	*Dinopium shorii*	
Black-rumped Flameback	*Dinopium benghalense*	
Pale-headed Woodpecker	*Gecinulus grantia*	CR
Rufous Woodpecker	*Micropternus brachyurus*	
Grey-headed woodpecker	*Picus canus*	
Greater Yellownape	*Chrysophlegma flavinucha*	
Lesser Yellownape	*Picus chlorolophus*	
Streak-throated Woodpecker	*Picus xanthopygaeus*	
Black-naped Woodpecker	*Picus guerini*	
Scaly-bellied Woodpecker	*Picus squamatus*	
Great Slaty Woodpecker	*Mulleripicus pulverulentus*	**VU**, EN
Grey-capped Pygmy Woodpecker	*Yungipicus canicapillus*	
Brown-capped Pygmy Woodpecker	*Yungipicus nanus*	
Yellow-crowned Woodpecker	*Leiopicus mahrattensis*	
Brown-fronted Woodpecker	*Leiopicus auriceps*	
Scarlet-breasted Woodpecker	*Dryobates cathpharius*	
Rufous-bellied Woodpecker	*Dendrocopos hyperythrus*	
Fulvous-breasted Woodpecker	*Dendrocopos macei*	
Darjeeling Woodpecker	*Dendrocopos darjellensis*	
Himalayan Woodpecker	*Dendrocopos himalayensis*	
CARIAMIFORMES		
Falconidae (Falcons & Caracras)		
Collared Falconet	*Microhierax caerulescens*	II
Lesser Kestrel	*Falco naumanni*	II
Common Kestrel	*Falco tinnunculus*	II
Red-headed Falcon	*Falco chicquera*	II, EN
Amur Falcon	*Falco amurensis*	II
Merlin	*Falco columbarius*	II
Eurasian Hobby	*Falco subbuteo*	II
Oriental Hobby	*Falco severus*	II, CR
Laggar Falcon	*Falco jugger*	I, CR
Saker Falcon	*Falco cherrug*	**EN**, II, EN
Peregrine Falcon	*Falco peregrinus*	I
PSITTACIFORMES		
Psittacidae (Parrots)		

Common English Name	Scientific Name	Status
Vernal Hanging-parrot	*Loriculus vernalis*	II, CR
Slaty-headed Parakeet	*Psittacula himalayana*	II
Blossom-headed Parakeet	*Psittacula roseata*	II
Plum-headed Parakeet	*Psittacula cyanocephala*	II
Red-breasted Parakeet	*Psittacula alexandri*	II, VU
Alexandrine Parakeet	*Psittacula eupatria*	II
Rose-ringed Parakeet	*Psittacula krameri*	
PASSERIFORMES		
Pittidae (Pittas)		
Blue-naped Pitta	*Hydrornis nipalensis*	EN
Indian Pitta	*Pitta brachyura*	
Western Hooded Pitta	*Pitta sordida*	VU
Eurylaimidae (Broadbills)		
Long-tailed Broadbill	*Psarisomus dalhousiae*	
Grey-browed Broadbill	*Serilophus rubropygius*	
Oriolidae (Orioles)		
Maroon Oriole	*Oriolus traillii*	
Black-hooded Oriole	*Oriolus xanthornus*	
Indian Golden Oriole	*Oriolus kundoo*	
Slender-billed Oriole	*Oriolus tenuirostris*	
Black-naped Oriole	*Oriolus chinensis*	
Vireonidae (Vireos)		
Black-headed Shrike-babbler	*Pteruthius rufiventer*	VU
White-browed Shrike-babbler	*Pteruthius aeralatus*	
Green Shrike-babbler	*Pteruthius xanthochlorus*	
Black-eared Shrike-babbler	*Pteruthius melanotis*	
White-bellied Erpornis	*Erpornis zantholeuca*	
Campephagidae (Cuckooshrikes & Allies)		
Small Minivet	*Pericrocotus cinnamomeus*	
Grey-chinned Minivet	*Pericrocotus solaris*	
Short-billed Minivet	*Pericrocotus brevirostris*	
Long-tailed Minivet	*Pericrocotus ethologus*	
Scarlet Minivet	*Pericrocotus flammeus*	
Rosy Minivet	*Pericrocotus roseus*	
Ashy Minivet	*Pericrocotus divaricatus*	
Swinhoe's Minivet	*Pericrocotus cantonensis*	
Indian Cuckooshrike	*Coracina macei*	
Black-winged Cuckooshrike	*Lalage melaschistos*	
Black-headed Cuckooshrike	*Lalage melanoptera*	
Artamidae (Woodswallows & Butcherbirds)		
Ashy Woodswallow	*Artamus fuscus*	
Vangidae (Vangas)		
Bar-winged Flycatcher-shrike	*Hemipus picatus*	
Large Woodshrike	*Tephrodornis virgatus*	
Common Woodshrike	*Tephrodornis pondicerianus*	
Aegithinidae (Ioras)		
Common Iora	*Aegithina tiphia*	
Rhipiduridae (Fantails)		
White-browed Fantail	*Rhipidura aureola*	
White-throated Fantail	*Rhipidura albicollis*	
Dicruridae (Drongos)		

Common English Name	Scientific Name	Status
Black Drongo	*Dicrurus macrocercus*	
Ashy Drongo	*Dicrurus leucophaeus*	
White-bellied Drongo	*Dicrurus caerulescens*	
Crow-billed Drongo	*Dicrurus annectens*	
Bronzed Drongo	*Dicrurus aeneus*	
Lesser Racquet-tailed Drongo	*Dicrurus remifer*	
Spangled Drongo	*Dicrurus hottentottus*	
Greater Racquet-tailed Drongo	*Dicrurus paradiseus*	
Monarchidae (Monarchs)		
Black-naped Monarch	*Hypothymis azurea*	
Indian Paradise-flycatcher	*Terpsiphone paradisi*	
Laniidae (Shrikes)		
Brown Shrike	*Lanius cristatus*	
Isabelline Shrike	*Lanius isabellinus*	
Bay-backed Shrike	*Lanius vittatus*	
Long-tailed Shrike	*Lanius schach*	
Grey-backed Shrike	*Lanius tephronotus*	
Great Grey Shrike	*Lanius excubitor*	CR
Corvidae (Crows)		
Rufous Treepie	*Dendrocitta vagabunda*	
Grey Treepie	*Dendrocitta formosae*	
Red-billed Chough	*Pyrrhocorax pyrrhocorax*	
Yellow-billed Chough	*Pyrrhocorax graculus*	
Yellow-billed Blue Magpie	*Urocissa flavirostris*	
Red-billed Blue Magpie	*Urocissa erythroryncha*	
Common Green Magpie	*Cissa chinensis*	
Eurasian Jay	*Garrulus glandarius*	EN
Black-headed Jay	*Garrulus lanceolatus*	
Spotted Nutcracker	*Nucifraga caryocatactes*	
Common Raven	*Corvus corax*	
House Crow	*Corvus splendens*	
Large-billed Crow	*Corvus macrorhynchos*	
Stenostiridae (Fairy Flycatchers & Allies)		
Yellow-bellied Fantail	*Chelidorhynx hypoxanthus*	
Grey-headed Canary-flycatcher	*Culicicapa ceylonensis*	
Paridae (Tits)		
Fire-capped Tit	*Cephalopyrus flammiceps*	
Yellow-browed Tit	*Sylviparus modestus*	
Sultan Tit	*Melanochlora sultanea*	EN
Coal Tit	*Periparus ater*	
Rufous-naped Tit	*Periparus rufonuchalis*	
Rufous-vented Tit	*Periparus rubidiventris*	
Grey-crested Tit	*Lophophanes dichrous*	
Ground Tit	*Pseudopodoces humilis*	
Green-backed Tit	*Parus monticolus*	
Great Tit	*Parus major*	
Black-lored Tit	*Machlolophus xanthogenys*	
Yellow-cheeked Tit	*Machlolophus spilonotus*	CR
Alaudidae (Larks)		
Rufous-tailed Lark	*Ammomanes phoenicura*	
Ashy-crowned Sparrow-lark	*Eremopterix griseus*	

Common English Name	Scientific Name	Status
Horsfield's Bushlark	*Mirafra javanica*	
Bengal Bushlark	*Mirafra assamica*	
Sand Lark	*Alaudala raytal*	
Hume's Lark	*Calandrella acutirostris*	
Eastern Short-toed Lark	*Calandrella dukhunensis*	
Horned Lark	*Eremophila alpestris*	
Oriental Skylark	*Alauda gulgula*	
Crested Lark	*Galerida cristata*	
Tibetan Lark	*Melanocorypha maxima*	
Eurasian Skylark	*Alauda arvensis*	
Cisticolidae (Cisticolas & Allies)		
Zitting Cisticola	*Cisticola juncidis*	
Golden-headed Cisticola	*Cisticola exilis*	
Striated Prinia	*Prinia crinigera*	
Black-throated Prinia	*Prinia atrogularis*	
Grey-crowned Prinia	*Prinia cinereocapilla*	**VU**, CR
Grey-breasted Prinia	*Prinia hodgsonii*	
Graceful Prinia	*Prinia gracilis*	
Jungle Prinia	*Prinia sylvatica*	
Yellow-bellied Prinia	*Prinia flaviventris*	
Ashy Prinia	*Prinia socialis*	
Plain Prinia	*Prinia inornata*	
Common Tailorbird	*Orthotomus sutorius*	
Acrocephalidae (Acrocephalid Warblers)		
Thick-billed Warbler	*Arundinax aedon*	
Booted Warbler	*Iduna caligata*	
Black-browed Reed Warbler	*Acrocephalus bistrigiceps*	
Blyth's Reed Warbler	*Acrocephalus dumetorum*	
Paddyfield Warbler	*Acrocephalus agricola*	
Blunt-winged Warbler	*Acrocephalus concinens*	
Clamorous Reed Warbler	*Acrocephalus stentoreus*	
Moustached Warbler	*Acrocephalus melanopogon*	
Oriental Reed Warbler	*Acrocephalus orientalis*	
Pnoepygidae (Wren-babblers)		
Nepal Cupwing	*Pnoepyga immaculata*	
Pygmy Cupwing	*Pnoepyga pusilla*	
Scaly-breasted Cupwing	*Pnoepyga albiventer*	
Locustellidae (Grassbirds & Allies)		
Pallas's Grasshopper Warbler	*Locustella certhiola*	
Lanceolated Warbler	*Locustella lanceolata*	
Brown Grasshopper Warbler	*Locustella luteoventris*	
Chinese Grasshopper Warbler	*Locustella tacsanowskia*	
Spotted Grasshopper Warbler	*Locustella thoracica*	
Himalayan Grasshopper Warbler	*Locustella kashmirensis*	
Common Grasshopper Warbler	*Locustella naevia*	
Baikal Grasshopper Warbler	*Locustella davidi*	
Striated Grassbird	*Megalurus palustris*	CR
Bristled Grassbird	*Chaetornis striata*	**VU**, VU
Hirundinidae (Swallows & Martins)		
Asian House Martin	*Delichon dasypus*	
Nepal House Martin	*Delichon nipalense*	
Northern House Martin	*Delichon urbicum*	

Common English Name	Scientific Name	Status
Streak-throated Swallow	*Petrochelidon fluvicola*	
Wire-tailed Swallow	*Hirundo smithii*	
Barn Swallow	*Hirundo rustica*	
Red-rumped Swallow	*Cecropis daurica*	
Eurasian Crag Martin	*Ptyonoprogne rupestris*	
Plain Martin	*Riparia paludicola*	
Collared Sand Martin	*Riparia riparia*	
Pale Sand Martin	*Riparia diluta*	
Pycnonotidae (Bulbuls)		
White-throated Bulbul	*Alophoixus flaveolus*	EN
Ashy Bulbul	*Hemixos flavala*	
Mountain Bulbul	*Ixos mcclellandii*	
Black Bulbul	*Hypsipetes leucocephalus*	
Striated Bulbul	*Pycnonotus striatus*	
Black-crested Bulbul	*Pycnonotus flaviventris*	
Red-whiskered Bulbul	*Pycnonotus jocosus*	
Himalayan Bulbul	*Pycnonotus leucogenys*	
Red-vented Bulbul	*Pycnonotus cafer*	
Scotocercidae (Bush Warblers)		
Asian Stubtail	*Urosphena squameiceps*	
Mountain Tailorbird	*Phyllergates cucullatus*	
Yellow-browed Warbler	*Phylloscopus inornatus*	
Hume's Leaf Warbler	*Phylloscopus humei*	
Lemon-rumped Leaf Warbler	*Phylloscopus chloronotus*	
Buff-barred Warbler	*Phylloscopus pulcher*	
Ashy-throated Warbler	*Phylloscopus maculipennis*	
Dusky Warbler	*Phylloscopus fuscatus*	
Smoky Warbler	*Phylloscopus fuligiventer*	
Siberian Chiffchaff	*Phylloscopus tristis*	
Tytler's Leaf Warbler	*Phylloscopus tytleri*	
Sulphur-bellied Warbler	*Phylloscopus griseolus*	
Tickell's Leaf Warbler	*Phylloscopus affinis*	
Grey-cheeked Warbler	*Phylloscopus poliogenys*	
Green-crowned Warbler	*Phylloscopus burkii*	
Whistler's Warbler	*Phylloscopus whistleri*	
Chestnut-crowned Warbler	*Phylloscopus castaniceps*	
Greenish Warbler	*Phylloscopus trochiloides*	
Large-billed Leaf Warbler	*Phylloscopus magnirostris*	
Yellow-vented Warbler	*Phylloscopus cantator*	EN
White-spectacled Warbler	*Phylloscopus intermedius*	
Blyth's Leaf Warbler	*Phylloscopus reguloides*	
Western Crowned Leaf Warbler	*Phylloscopus occipitalis*	
Grey-hooded Warbler	*Phylloscopus xanthoschistos*	
Radde's Warbler	*Phylloscopus schwarzi*	
Green Warbler	*Phylloscopus nitidus*	
Slaty-bellied Tesia	*Tesia olivea*	CR
Grey-bellied Tesia	*Tesia cyaniventer*	
Chestnut-headed Tesia	*Cettia castaneocoronata*	
Chestnut-crowned Bush Warbler	*Cettia major*	
Grey-sided Bush Warbler	*Cettia brunnifrons*	
Pale-footed Bush Warbler	*Cettia pallidipes*	VU
Yellow-bellied Warbler	*Abroscopus superciliaris*	VU

Common English Name	Scientific Name	Status
Rufous-faced Warbler	*Abroscopus albogularis*	CR
Black-faced Warbler	*Abroscopus schisticeps*	
Broad-billed Warbler	*Tickellia hodgsoni*	EN
Brownish-flanked Bush Warbler	*Horornis fortipes*	
Hume's Bush Warbler	*Horornis brunnescens*	VU
Aberrant Bush Warbler	*Horornis flavolivaceus*	
Aegithalidae (Bushtits)		
White-browed Tit-warbler	*Leptopoecile sophiae*	
Black-throated Tit	*Aegithalos concinnus*	
White-throated Tit	*Aegithalos niveogularis*	
Rufous-fronted Tit	*Aegithalos iouschistos*	
Sylviidae (Old World Warblers)		
Lesser Whitethroat	*Sylvia curruca*	
Eastern Orphean Warbler	*Sylvia crassirostris*	
Fire-tailed Myzornis	*Myzornis pyrrhoura*	
Golden-breasted Fulvetta	*Lioparus chrysotis*	VU
Yellow-eyed Babbler	*Chrysomma sinense*	
Jerdon's Babbler	*Chrysomma altirostre*	**VU**, CR
White-browed Fulvetta	*Fulvetta vinipectus*	
Great Parrotbill	*Conostoma aemodium*	VU
Brown Parrotbill	*Cholornis unicolor*	VU
Fulvous Parrotbill	*Suthora fulvifrons*	VU
Black-throated Parrotbill	*Suthora nipalensis*	
Black-breasted Parrotbill	*Paradoxornis flavirostris*	**VU**
Zosteropidae (White-eyes)		
Black-chinned Yuhina	*Yuhina nigrimenta*	VU
Stripe-throated Yuhina	*Yuhina gularis*	
Whiskered Yuhina	*Yuhina flavicollis*	
Rufous-vented Yuhina	*Yuhina occipitalis*	
White-naped Yuhina	*Yuhina bakeri*	CR
Oriental White-eye	*Zosterops palpebrosus*	
Timaliidae (Old World Babblers)		
Rufous-throated Wren Babbler	*Spelaeornis caudatus*	CR
Blackish-breasted Babbler	*Stachyris humei*	CR
Coral-billed Scimitar Babbler	*Pomatorhinus ferruginosus*	CR
Slender-billed Scimitar Babbler	*Pomatorhinus superciliaris*	VU
White-browed Scimitar Babbler	*Pomatorhinus schisticeps*	
Streak-breasted Scimitar Babbler	*Pomatorhinus ruficollis*	
Rusty-cheeked Scimitar Babbler	*Pomatorhinus erythrogenys*	
Grey-throated Babbler	*Stachyris nigriceps*	
Tawny-bellied Babbler	*Dumetia hyperythra*	EN
Chestnut-capped Babbler	*Timalia pileata*	
Pin-striped Tit Babbler	*Macronus gularis*	
Golden Babbler	*Cyanoderma chrysaeum*	EN
Black-chinned Babbler	*Cyanoderma pyrrhops*	
Rufous-capped Babbler	*Cyanoderma ruficeps*	
Pellorneidae (Jungle Babblers)		
White-hooded Babbler	*Gampsorhynchus rufulus*	CR
Rufous-winged Fulvetta	*Schoeniparus castaneceps*	
Swamp Grass-babbler	*Laticilla cinerascens*	**EN**, CR
Puff-throated Babbler	*Pellorneum ruficeps*	
Abbott's Babbler	*Malacocincla abbotti*	EN

Common English Name	Scientific Name	Status
Long-billed Wren-babbler	*Rimator malacoptilus*	
Indian Grass-babbler	*Graminicola bengalensis*	EN
Leiotrichidae (Laughingthrushes)		
Nepal Fulvetta	*Alcippe nipalensis*	
Himalayan Cutia	*Cutia nipalensis*	
Striated Babbler	*Argya earlei*	
Common Babbler	*Argya caudata*	VU
Spiny Babbler	*Turdoides nipalensis*	
Slender-billed Babbler	*Chatarrhaea longirostris*	**VU**, CR
Jungle Babbler	*Turdoides striata*	
Large Grey Babbler	*Turdoides malcolmi*	
Striated Laughingthrush	*Grammatoptila striatus*	
Lesser Necklaced Laughingthrush	*Garrulax monileger*	VU
Greater Necklaced Laughingthrush	*Garrulax pectoralis*	VU
White-crested Laughingthrush	*Garrulax leucolophus*	
Spotted Laughingthrush	*Garrulax ocellatus*	
Rufous-chinned Laughingthrush	*Garrulax rufogularis*	
White-throated Laughingthrush	*Garrulax albogularis*	
Grey-sided Laughingthrush	*Garrulax caerulatus*	VU
Rufous-necked Laughingthrush	*Garrulax ruficollis*	CR
Scaly Laughingthrush	*Trochalopteron subunicolor*	
Blue-winged Laughingthrush	*Trochalopteron squamatum*	
Streaked Laughingthrush	*Trochalopteron lineatum*	
Variegated Laughingthrush	*Trochalopteron variegatum*	
Black-faced Laughingthrush	*Trochalopteron affine*	
Chestnut-crowned Laughingthrush	*Trochalopteron erythrocephalum*	
Long-tailed Sibia	*Heterophasia picaoides*	CR
Rufous Sibia	*Heterophasia capistrata*	
Silver-eared Mesia	*Leiothrix argentauris*	II, EN
Red-billed Leiothrix	*Leiothrix lutea*	II
Rufous-backed Sibia	*Leioptila annectens*	CR
Red-tailed Minla	*Minla ignotincta*	
Red-faced Liocichla	*Liocichla phoenicea*	
Hoary-throated Barwing	*Sibia nipalensis*	
Blue-winged Minla	*Siva cyanouroptera*	
Bar-throated Minla	*Chrysominla strigula*	
Rusty-fronted Barwing	*Actinodura egertoni*	EN
Certhiidae (Treecreepers)		
Rusty-flanked Treecreeper	*Certhia nipalensis*	
Sikkim Treecreeper	*Certhia discolor*	
Bar-tailed Treecreeper	*Certhia himalayana*	
Hodgson's Treecreeper	*Certhia hodgsoni*	
Sittidae (Nuthatches)		
Kashmir Nuthatch	*Sitta cashmirensis*	
Indian Nuthatch	*Sitta castanea*	
Chestnut-bellied Nuthatch	*Sitta cinnamoventris*	
White-tailed Nuthatch	*Sitta himalayensis*	
White-cheeked Nuthatch	*Sitta leucopsis*	
Velvet-fronted Nuthatch	*Sitta frontalis*	
Wallcreeper	*Tichodroma muraria*	
Troglodytidae (Wrens)		
Northern Wren	*Troglodytes troglodytes*	

Common English Name	Scientific Name	Status
Cinclidae (Dippers)		
White-throated Dipper	*Cinclus cinclus*	
Brown Dipper	*Cinclus pallasii*	
Sturnidae (Starlings & Mynas)		
Common Starling	*Sturnus vulgaris*	
Rosy Starling	*Pastor roseus*	
Asian Pied Starling	*Gracupica contra*	
Brahminy Starling	*Sturnia pagodarum*	
Chestnut-tailed Starling	*Sturnia malabarica*	
White-shouldered Starling	*Sturnia sinensis*	
Common Myna	*Acridotheres tristis*	
Bank Myna	*Acridotheres ginginianus*	
Jungle Myna	*Acridotheres fuscus*	
Great Myna	*Acridotheres grandis*	
Spot-winged Starling	*Saroglossa spilopterus*	
Common Hill Myna	*Gracula religiosa*	II
Purple-backed Starling	*Agropsar sturninus*	
Asian Glossy Starling	*Aplonis panayensis*	
Turdidae (Thrushes)		
Grandala	*Grandala coelicolor*	
Long-tailed Thrush	*Zoothera dixoni*	
Alpine Thrush	*Zoothera mollissima*	
Dark-sided Thrush	*Zoothera marginata*	VU
Long-billed Thrush	*Zoothera monticola*	
Scaly Thrush	*Zoothera dauma*	
Purple Cochoa	*Cochoa purpurea*	EN
Green Cochoa	*Cochoa viridis*	
Pied Thrush	*Geokichla wardii*	
Orange-headed Thrush	*Geokichla citrina*	
Mistle Thrush	*Turdus viscivorus*	
Grey-winged Blackbird	*Turdus boulboul*	
Tickell's Thrush	*Turdus unicolor*	
Tibetan Blackbird	*Turdus maximus*	
White-collared Blackbird	*Turdus albocinctus*	
Chestnut Thrush	*Turdus rubrocanus*	
Dusky Thrush	*Turdus eunomus*	
Black-throated Thrush	*Turdus atrogularis*	
Rufous-throated Thrush	*Turdus ruficollis*	
Eyebrowed Thrush	*Turdus obscurus*	
White-backed Thrush	*Turdus kessleri*	
Grey-sided Thrush	*Turdus feae*	**VU**
Muscicapidae (Old World Flycatchers)		
Oriental Magpie Robin	*Copsychus saularis*	
Indian Robin	*Saxicoloides fulicatus*	
White-rumped Shama	*Copsychus malabaricus*	
Dark-sided Flycatcher	*Muscicapa sibirica*	
Asian Brown Flycatcher	*Muscicapa dauurica*	
Brown-breasted Flycatcher	*Muscicapa muttui*	
Ferruginous Flycatcher	*Muscicapa ferruginea*	
Rufous-bellied Niltava	*Niltava sundara*	
Small Niltava	*Niltava macgrigoriae*	
Large Niltava	*Niltava grandis*	

Common English Name	Scientific Name	Status
Verditer Flycatcher	Eumyias thalassinus	
White-gorgeted Flycatcher	Anthipes monileger	VU
Pale Blue Flycatcher	Cyornis unicolor	
Pale-chinned Flycatcher	Cyornis poliogenys	
Tickell's Blue Flycatcher	Cyornis tickelliae	
Blue-throated Blue Flycatcher	Cyornis rubeculoides	
Gould's Shortwing	Heteroxenicus stellatus	EN
Lesser Shortwing	Brachypteryx leucophris	
Himalayan Shortwing	Brachypteryx cruralis	
Indian Blue Robin	Larvivora brunnea	
Siberian Blue Robin	Larvivora cyane	
White-bellied Redstart	Hodgsonius phaenicuroides	
Bluethroat	Cyanecula svecica	
Siberian Rubythroat	Calliope calliope	
White-tailed Rubythroat	Calliope pectoralis	
Chinese Rubythroat	Calliope tschebaiewi	
White-tailed Blue Robin	Myiomela leucura	
Rufous-breasted Bush-robin	Tarsiger hyperythrus	
Himalayan Bush-robin	Tarsiger rufilatus	
White-browed Bush-robin	Tarsiger indicus	
Golden Bush-robin	Tarsiger chrysaeus	
Little Forktail	Enicurus scouleri	
Slaty-backed Forktail	Enicurus schistaceus	
Black-backed Forktail	Enicurus immaculatus	
Spotted Forktail	Enicurus maculatus	
Blue Whistling Thrush	Myophonus caeruleus	
Slaty-backed Flycatcher	Ficedula erithacus	
Slaty-blue Flycatcher	Ficedula tricolor	
Snowy-browed Flycatcher	Ficedula hyperythra	
Pygmy Blue Flycatcher	Ficedula hodgsoni	
Rufous-gorgeted Flycatcher	Ficedula strophiata	
Sapphire Flycatcher	Ficedula sapphira	
Ultramarine Flycatcher	Ficedula superciliaris	
Little Pied Flycatcher	Ficedula westermanni	
Rusty-tailed Flycatcher	Ficedula ruficauda	
Red-throated Flycatcher	Ficedula albicilla	
Red-breasted Flycatcher	Ficedula parva	
Kashmir Flycatcher	Ficedula subrubra	**VU**, VU
Eversmann's Redstart	Phoenicurus erythronotus	
Blue-fronted Redstart	Phoenicurus frontalis	
Blue-capped Redstart	Phoenicurus coeruleocephala	
White-throated Redstart	Phoenicurus schisticeps	
White-capped Water Redstart	Phoenicurus leucocephalus	
Plumbeous Water Redstart	Phoenicurus fuliginosus	
Black Redstart	Phoenicurus ochruros	
White-winged Redstart	Phoenicurus erythrogastrus	
Hodgson's Redstart	Phoenicurus hodgsoni	
Daurian Redstart	Phoenicurus auroreus	
Blue-capped Rock Thrush	Monticola cinclorhyncha	
Chestnut-bellied Rock Thrush	Monticola rufiventris	
Blue Rock Thrush	Monticola solitarius	
Rufous-tailed Rock Thrush	Monticola saxatilis	

Common English Name	Scientific Name	Status
Jerdon's Bushchat	*Saxicola jerdoni*	CR
Grey Bushchat	*Saxicola ferreus*	
White-throated Bushchat	*Saxicola insignis*	**VU**, EN
Pied Bushchat	*Saxicola caprata*	
White-tailed Stonechat	*Saxicola leucurus*	
Common Stonechat	*Saxicola torquatus*	
Northern Wheatear	*Oenanthe oenanthe*	
Isabelline Wheatear	*Oenanthe isabellina*	
Pied Wheatear	*Oenanthe pleschanka*	
Variable Wheatear	*Oenanthe picata*	
Red-tailed Wheatear	*Oenanthe chrysopygia*	
Desert Wheatear	*Oenanthe deserti*	
Brown Rockchat	*Oenanthe fusca*	
Regulidae (Kinglets)		
Goldcrest	*Regulus regulus*	
Bombycillidae (Waxwings)		
Bohemian Waxwing	*Bombycilla garrulus*	
Elachuridae (Spotted Wren-babbler)		
Spotted Elachura	*Elachura formosa*	CR
Irenidae (Fairy Bluebirds)		
Asian Fairy Bluebird	*Irena puella*	CR
Chloropseidae (Leafbirds)		
Golden-fronted Leafbird	*Chloropsis aurifrons*	
Orange-bellied Leafbird	*Chloropsis hardwickii*	
Dicaeidae (Flowerpeckers)		
Yellow-bellied Flowerpecker	*Dicaeum melanozanthum*	
Yellow-vented Flowerpecker	*Dicaeum chrysorrheum*	CR
Thick-billed Flowerpecker	*Dicaeum agile*	
Pale-billed Flowerpecker	*Dicaeum erythrorhynchos*	
Plain Flowerpecker	*Dicaeum minullum*	
Scarlet-backed Flowerpecker	*Dicaeum cruentatum*	CR
Fire-breasted Flowerpecker	*Dicaeum ignipectus*	
Nectariniidae (Sunbirds & Spiderhunters)		
Little Spiderhunter	*Arachnothera longirostra*	CR
Streaked Spiderhunter	*Arachnothera magna*	
Ruby-cheeked Sunbird	*Chalcoparia singalensis*	EN
Purple Sunbird	*Cinnyris asiaticus*	
Fire-tailed Sunbird	*Aethopyga ignicauda*	
Black-throated Sunbird	*Aethopyga saturata*	
Green-tailed Sunbird	*Aethopyga nipalensis*	
Gould's Sunbird	*Aethopyga gouldiae*	
Crimson Sunbird	*Aethopyga siparaja*	
Prunellidae (Accentors)		
Altai Accentor	*Prunella himalayana*	
Alpine Accentor	*Prunella collaris*	
Maroon-backed Accentor	*Prunella immaculata*	
Robin Accentor	*Prunella rubeculoides*	
Rufous-breasted Accentor	*Prunella strophiata*	
Brown Accentor	*Prunella fulvescens*	
Black-throated Accentor	*Prunella atrogularis*	
Ploceidae (Weavers)		
Black-breasted Weaver	*Ploceus benghalensis*	VU

Common English Name	Scientific Name	Status
Streaked Weaver	*Ploceus manyar*	CR
Baya Weaver	*Ploceus philippinus*	
Finn's Weaver	*Ploceus megarhynchus*	*VU*, CR
Estrildidae (Estrilid Finches)		
Red Avadavat	*Amandava amandava*	
Indian Silverbill	*Euodice malabarica*	
White-rumped Munia	*Lonchura striata*	
Scaly-breasted Munia	*Lonchura punctulata*	
Chestnut Munia	*Lonchura atricapilla*	EN
Black-headed Munia	*Lonchura malacca*	
Passeridae (Old World Sparrows)		
House Sparrow	*Passer domesticus*	
Russet Sparrow	*Passer cinnamomeus*	
Eurasian Tree Sparrow	*Passer montanus*	
Chestnut-shouldered Bush- sparrow	*Gymnoris xanthocollis*	
Spanish Sparrow	*Passer hispaniolensis*	
Tibetan Snowfinch	*Montifringilla adamsi*	
White-rumped Snowfinch	*Onychostruthus taczanowskii*	
Rufous-necked Snowfinch	*Pyrgilauda ruficollis*	
Plain-backed Snowfinch	*Pyrgilauda blanfordi*	
Motacillidae (Pipits & Wagtails)		
Tree Pipit	*Anthus trivialis*	
Olive-backed Pipit	*Anthus hodgsoni*	
Red-throated Pipit	*Anthus cervinus*	
Rosy Pipit	*Anthus roseatus*	
Water Pipit	*Anthus spinoletta*	
Upland Pipit	*Anthus sylvanus*	
Richard's Pipit	*Anthus richardi*	
Paddyfield Pipit	*Anthus rufulus*	
Blyth's Pipit	*Anthus godlewskii*	
Long-billed Pipit	*Anthus similis*	
Tawny Pipit	*Anthus campestris*	
Buff-bellied Pipit	*Anthus rubescens*	
Yellow Wagtail	*Motacilla flava*	
Grey Wagtail	*Motacilla cinerea*	
Citrine Wagtail	*Motacilla citreola*	
White-browed Wagtail	*Motacilla maderaspatensis*	
White Wagtail	*Motacilla alba*	
Forest Wagtail	*Dendronanthus indicus*	
Fringillidae (Finches)		
Common Chaffinch	*Fringilla coelebs*	
Brambling	*Fringilla montifringilla*	
Black-and-yellow Grosbeak	*Mycerobas icterioides*	
Collared Grosbeak	*Mycerobas affinis*	
Spot-winged Grosbeak	*Mycerobas melanozanthos*	
White-winged Grosbeak	*Mycerobas carnipes*	
Common Rosefinch	*Carpodacus erythrinus*	
Scarlet Finch	*Carpodacus sipahi*	
Beautiful Rosefinch	*Carpodacus pulcherrimus*	
Dark-rumped Rosefinch	*Carpodacus edwardsii*	
Pink-browed Rosefinch	*Carpodacus rodochroa*	
Spot-winged Rosefinch	*Carpodacus rodopeplus*	

Common English Name	Scientific Name	Status
Vinaceous Rosefinch	*Carpodacus vinaceus*	
Streaked Rosefinch	*Carpodacus rubicilloides*	
Great Rosefinch	*Carpodacus rubicilla*	
Red-fronted Rosefinch	*Carpodacus puniceus*	
Crimson-browed Finch	*Carpodacus subhimachalus*	
White-browed Rosefinch	*Carpodacus thura*	
Brown Bullfinch	*Pyrrhula nipalensis*	
Red-headed Bullfinch	*Pyrrhula erythrocephala*	
Grey-headed Bullfinch	*Pyrrhula erythaca*	
Mongolian Finch	*Bucanetes mongolicus*	
Blanford's Rosefinch	*Agraphospiza rubescens*	
Spectacled Finch	*Callacanthis burtoni*	
Gold-naped Finch	*Pyrrhoplectes epauletta*	VU
Dark-breasted Rosefinch	*Procarduelis nipalensis*	
Plain Mountain Finch	*Leucosticte nemoricola*	
Brandt's Mountain Finch	*Leucosticte brandti*	
Yellow-breasted Greenfinch	*Chloris spinoides*	
Twite	*Linaria flavirostris*	
Red Crossbill	*Loxia curvirostra*	
Eastern Goldfinch	*Carduelis caniceps*	
Red-fronted Serin	*Serinus pusillus*	
Tibetan Siskin	*Spinus thibetanus*	VU
Common Linnet	*Linaria cannabina*	
Eurasian Siskin	*Spinus spinus*	
Emberizidae (Buntings)		
Crested Bunting	*Emberiza lathami*	
Black-headed Bunting	*Emberiza melanocephala*	VU
Red-headed Bunting	*Emberiza bruniceps*	
Chestnut-eared Bunting	*Emberiza fucata*	
Rock Bunting	*Emberiza cia*	
Pine Bunting	*Emberiza leucocephalos*	
Yellow-breasted Bunting	*Emberiza aureola*	**CR**, CR
Little Bunting	*Emberiza pusilla*	VU
Black-faced Bunting	*Emberiza spodocephala*	VU
Chestnut Bunting	*Emberiza rutila*	
Yellowhammer	*Emberiza citrinella*	
Grey-necked Bunting	*Emberiza buchanani*	
White-capped Bunting	*Emberiza stewarti*	
Rustic Bunting	*Emberiza rustica*	**VU**
Reed Bunting	*Schoeniclus schoeniclus*	

Further Reading

Ali, S. (1941) *The Book of Indian Birds*. Bombay: BNHS.

Ali, S. (1960) *A Picture Book of Sikkim Birds*. Gangtok : Government of Sikkim.

Ali, S. (1962) *The Birds of Sikkim*. Delhi: OUP.

Ali, S. & Ripley, D. (1964–74) *Handbook of the Birds of India & Pakistan* (Vols. 1–10). Bombay: OUP.

Ali, S. (1977) *Field Guide to the Birds of the Eastern Himalayas*. Bombay: OUP.

Ali, S. & Ripley, D. (1983) *A Pictorial Guide to the Birds of the Indian Subcontinent*. Bombay: OUP.

Ali, S., Biswas, B. & Ripley, D. (1996) *Birds of Bhutan*. Calcutta: ZSI.

Baker, E. C. S. (1913) *Indian Pigeons and Doves*. London: Witherby & Co.

Beebe, W. (1927, 1994) *Pheasant Jungles*. Reading: WPA.

Dewar, D. (1915) *Birds of the Indian Hills*. London: The Bodley Head.

Fleming, R. L. Sr. & Fleming, R. Jr. (1970) *Birds of Kathmandu and Surrounding Hills*. Kathmandu: Jore Ganesh Press.

Fleming, R. L. Sr. et al. (1984) *Birds of Nepal: With reference to Kashmir and Sikkim*. Nepal: Nature Himalayas.

Gould, J. (1832) *A Century of Birds from the Himalayan Mountains*. London: Published by the author.

Grewal, B. (1995) *Birds of the Indian Subcontinent*. Hong Kong: The Guidebook Company Limited.

Grewal, B. (1995, 2008) *Birds of the India & Nepal*. London: New Holland.

Grewal, B. (1998) *A Photographic Guide to the Birds of the Himalayas*. London: New Holland.

Grewal, B., Pfister, O. & Harvey, B. (2002) *A Photographic Guide to the Birds of India, and the Indian Subcontinent including Pakistan, Nepal, Bhutan, Bangladesh, Sri Lanka and the Maldives*. Singapore: Periplus

Grimmet, R. Inskipp, T., & Inskipp, C. (1998) *Birds of the Indian Subcontinent*. UK: A&C Black.

Grimmet, R. Inskipp, T., & Inskipp, C. (1999) *Field Guide to the Birds of Bhutan*. UK: A&C Black.

Grimmet, R. Inskipp, T., & Inskipp, C. (2000) *Field Guide to the Birds of Nepal*. UK: A&C Black.

Inglis, C. M. (undated) *Sixty-eight Indian Birds*. Darjeeling: Natural History Museum.

Inskipp, C. (1988) *A Birdwatcher's Guide To Nepal*. England: Prion.

Inskipp, C. (1989) *Nepal's Forest Birds: Their Status and Conservation*. Cambridge: UK.

Inskipp, T. & Inskipp, C. (1991) *A Guide to The Birds of Nepal*. London: Christopher Helm.

Kazmierczak, K. & van Perlo, B. (2000) *A Field-Guide to the Birds of the Indian Subcontinent*. UK: Pica Press.

King, B. et al. (1991) *A Field Guide to the Birds of South East Asia*. London: Collins.

Mackintosh, L. J. (1915) *Birds of Darjeeling and India*: Part I. Calcutta: J. N. Banerjee & Son.

Murray, J. A. (1888) *Indian Birds or the Avifauna of British India*. Vols. I–2. London: Trubner & Co.

Murray, J. A. (1890) *The Avifauna of the Island of Ceylon*. Bombay: Educational Society Press.

Naoroji, R. (2006) *Birds of Prey of the Indian Subcontinent*. London: Christopher Helm.

Oates, E. W. (1899) *A Manual of the Game Birds of India*: Game Birds. Bombay: A. J. Combridge.

Pande, S., Tambe, S., Clement, Francis & Sant, N. (2003) *Birds of Western Ghats, Konkan and Malabar Mumbai*: BNHS.

Pfister, O. (2004) *Birds and Mammals of Ladakh*. New Delhi: OUP.

Phillips, W. W. A. (1949–1961) *Birds of Ceylon*: (Vols.1–4). Colombo: Ceylon Daily News Press, Lake House.

Rasmussen, P. & Anderton, J. (2005) *Birds of South Asia: The Ripley Guide*. Barcelona: Lynx Editions.

Ripley, D. (1952) *Search for the Spiny Babbler*. Boston: Houghton Mifflin.

Shrestha, T. K. (1998) *The Spiny Babbler, An Endemic Bird of Nepal*.

Vaurie, Charles. (1972) *Tibet and its Birds*. London: H. F. & G. Witherby Ltd.

Woodcock, M. (1980) *Collins Handguide to the Birds of the Indian Subcontinent*. London: Collins.

Sound Guides

Barucha, E. (1999) *Indian Bird Calls*. Bombay: BNHS.

Breil, F. & Roche, J. C. (2000) *Birding in India and Nepal*. Sittelle Editions.

Connop, S. (1993) *Birdsongs of Nepal*. New York: Turaco.

Connop, S. (1995) *Birdsongs of the Himalayas*. Toronto: Turaco.

White, T. (1984) *A Field Guide to the Bird Songs of South East Asia*. London: British Library.

Accentor, Robin 143
  Rufous-breasted 143
Accipiter badius 29
Acridotheres fuscus 113
  ginginianus 114
Acrocephalus agricola 96
  stentoreus 95
Actitis hypoleucos 42
Adjutant, Greater 20
  Lesser 19
Aegithalos concinnus 87
Aegithina tiphia 74
Aethopyga gouldiae 136
  nipalensis 137
  siparaja 137
Alcedo atthis 62
Alcippe nipalensis 109
Alectoris chukar 13
Amandava amandava 141
Anastomus oscitans 19
Anhinga melanogaster 23
Anthracoceros albirostris 66
Anthus hodgsoni 146
  rufulus 145
Antigone antigone 35
Aquila chrysaetos 33
  fasciata 32
  nipalensis 31
Arachnothera longirostra 138
Arborophila rufogularis 15
  torqueola 14
Argya caudata 103
  earlei 103
Athene brama 57
Avadavat, Red 141
Avocet, Pied 43
Babbler, Common 103
  Large Grey 104
  Puff-throated 102
  Spiny 104
  Striated 103
  Tawny-bellied 101
Barbet, Blue-throated 67
  Brown-headed 67
  Coppersmith 68
  Great 66
Bee-eater, Blue-bearded 63
  Chestnut-headed 64
  Green 63
Bittern, Black 23
Blackbird, Tibetan 118

Bubo b. bengalensis 56
Buceros bicornis 65
Bulbul, Black 90
  Black-crested 88
  Himalayan 90
  Mountain 89
  Red-vented 89
  Red-whiskered 88
Bullfinch, Red-headed 149
Bunting, Crested 151
  Grey-necked 150
  Rock 150
  White-capped 151
Bushchat, Grey 126
  Pied 125
Bush Warbler, Grey-sided 93
Butastur teesa 30
Buzzard, White-eyed 30
Calliope pectoralis 119
Caprimulgus affinis 58
  asiaticus 58
Carduelis caniceps 147
Carpodacus erythrinus 148
  thura 148
Cecropis daurica 92
Centropus sinensis 55
Cephalopyrus flammiceps 87
Certhia himalayana 112
Ceryle rudis 62
Cettia brunnifrons 93
  castaneocoronata 93
Chalcophaps indica 49
Charadrius dubius 38
Chloropsis aurifrons 133
Chrysocolaptes guttacristatus 73
Chrysophlegma flavinucha 71
Chukar 13
Ciconia episcopus 21
  nigra 20
Cinnyris asiaticus 136
Circus aeruginosus 29
Cisticola juncidis 97
Cisticola, Zitting 97
Clamator jacobinus 54
Clanga clanga 30
Collared Dove, Eurasian 50
  Red 51
Columba hodgsoni 47
  leuconota 47
  pulchricollis 46
  rupestris 46

Copsychus malabaricus 121
  saularis 120
Coracias benghalensis 60
Cormorant, Great 24
  Little 24
Corvus macrorhynchos 84
Coucal, Greater 55
Courser, Indian 44
Crag Martin, Eurasian 91
Crane, Black-necked 36
  Demoiselle 35
  Sarus 35
Crow, Large-billed 84
Cuckoo, Indian 55
  Jacobin 54
Cuculus micropterus 55
Curlew, Eurasian 40
Cursorius coromandelicus 44
Cyornis tickelliae 132
Darter, Oriental 23
Delichon nipalense 92
Dendrocitta vagabunda 83
Dendrocopos himalayensis 70
Dicaeum agile 134
  cruentatum 135
  erythrorhynchos 134
  ignipectus 135
Dicrurus hottentottus 79
  macrocercus 79
  paradiseus 80
Dinopium benghalense 72
Dove, Emerald 49
  Laughing 50
  Spotted 49
Drongo, Black 79
  Greater Racquet-tailed 80
  Spangled 79
Dumetia hyperythra 101
Eagle, Bonelli's 32
  Booted 32
  Golden 33
  Steppe 31
Eagle Owl, Indian 56
Elanus caeruleus 25
Emberiza buchanani 150
  cia 150
  stewarti 151
Enicurus maculatus 124
  scouleri 124
Eudynamys scolopaceus 54
Eumyias thalassinus 131